To

Phillips Memorial Baptist
Church

With
Regards

Jedi Johnston
8/31/99

(sister of Henry Forte)

.

Patriarch

Jodi Johnston

Noble House
Baltimore, Maryland

Patriarch

Copyright © 1994 Jodi Johnston

Library of Congress
Cataloging in Publication Data
ISBN 1-56167-148-7

Published by

Noble House

8019 Belair Road, Suite 10
Baltimore, Maryland 21236

Manufactured in the United States of America

I will lift up mine
eyes unto the hills,
from whence cometh my
help.
My help cometh from
the Lord, who made
heaven and earth . . .
~ Psalm 121 ~

Prologue

The peoples of the United States of America can best be described as a mosaic of immigrants and their descendants. America is thought of as unique because of this fact of her history. But, if one goes back in history to see how many other countries were settled and developed, the same pattern of migrating groups of people gathering and starting towns and villages is seen. The difference lies in the length of years that make up the history of different countries. The more years that a country has been in existence the more her identity becomes thought of as peoples of one ethnic group.

A turning point in the history of America was from the eighteen hundreds into the early nineteen hundreds. During this period there was an extensive and diverse influx of immigrants to America's shores and these people played a large role in shaping the identity of America. The railroad system that stretched across the some three thousand miles of America's land was built by immigrant laborers and they provided the labor for many of the farms and businesses that were created and built. They also started farms and businesses themselves. The majority of these migrating people to the shores of America had one thing in common. They were looking for opportunity and a better way of life for themselves and their families. Most of them had limited resources when they arrived but they were willing to work and build toward their dreams. Many had been craftsmen and artisans in the land from which they had come and they brought their talents and skills with them.

Their moral values, religious values and strong family ties contributed to the development of, and set the standards for, American society for years to come. It gave America a strong foundation upon which to grow, expand and to become the powerful nation that she is today. The diversity of these peoples allowed America to absorb the strength of the different ethnic groups and the different cultures from which they had come. And America in turn influenced these people and added new dimensions to their lives.

This melding of peoples from all corners of the earth into American society has produced a new 'ethnic group' based on diversity of people rather than any one heritage being dominant. This experience of her people has been good for them and good for the country that they call home. Their children and grandchildren and great-grandchildren have become Americans, members of a society based on diversity. The intermarriage of these descendants of the early immigrants has further melded the different cultural and ethnic backgrounds into what we now call Americans.

America's strength today is based on the history of her beginnings. The strength that came from the diversity of her early population and the melding of their descendants. Thomas J. Haddy was one of these early immigrants that came to the shores of the United States of America.

I

The soft black velvet sky stretched from horizon to horizon. It was ablaze with the bright sparkling stars that were splattered across its breath. Joseph Assaf El Haddy awoke and gazed at the splendor of the sky stretched above him. The ground, on which he was lying, was damp with the dew of the hot humid summer night. He got to his feet and gazed to the eastern horizon where a band of light stretched, and he knew that the dawn would soon be upon him. As he gazed at the breaking dawn his thoughts turned to his wife Tafiha, down in the village below, who was expecting their first child. He shivered with excitement at the thought of becoming a father and as any good Lebanese man hoped that the child would be a boy to carry on the family name. He looked over at his hired man, Hamid, who assisted him in tending his flock of goats on the hillside of Ain Arab, Lebanon, his home village. He walked over to Hamid and shook him to awaken him. Hamid stood and Joseph asked him to watch the flock as he wished to return to the village below to check on his wife's well-being. As he walked down the hillside, on this fifteenth day of July in 1892, his thoughts turned to his ancestry, the ancestry of this yet to be born child.

The name of El Haddy had been in the family of Joseph Assaf El Haddy since the year 1790. In the early eighteen hundreds one George El Haddy had married Hedla El Assis and they had been blessed with four sons. Kelled, born in 1816; Ead, born in 1819; Abusumra, born in 1822; and Assaf, born in 1825. All were born in Ain Arab, Lebanon. In 1860 Assaf El Haddy married Dellie Kamas, who had been born in 1845 in Kefarkook, Lebanon. Assaf and Dellie had four sons and a daughter. Joseph, born in 1866; Thomas, born in 1869; Freda, born in 1873; John, born in 1877; and Michael, born in 1881. All were born in Ain Arab, Lebanon. Assaf's life span would end in 1915 and Dellie's would end in 1925. They had lost two of their children while they were still in their childhood, Thomas and Freda. Their sons were goatherders in the hills above Ain Arab, Lebanon and they earned their living by raising goats and selling the milk, cheese, and meat that their herd provided. The El Haddy families were hardworking and respected members of their village.

As he walked down the same hillside where his ancestors had tended their flocks before him, Joseph, son of Assaf and Dellie, reflected with pride on his ancestry. The family pride that would be carried on by his soon to be born child. The pride also honored by his wife Tafiha, who had been born in 1872, the daughter of Abdulla Nemer Attyia of Ain Arab and whom Joseph had married in 1890.

Joseph approached the village and as he neared his home he saw several of the village women gathered around the door. He knew immediately that the mid-wife was there and his child was arriving. He excitedly broke into a run and within a few minutes was at the door of his home. As he arrived, the women shouted joyfully that he was the father of a healthy baby boy. Joseph also gave a shout of joy and hurried into the house as a wave of excitement washed over him. As he crossed the threshold he was greeted by his new son's howls. He strode across the room to where his wife was lying and looked down at the infant. The infant's fists were clenched, his face was beet red and he shrieked in indignation at the discomfort to which he was being subjected. A few minutes earlier he had been comfortably encased in his mother's womb and suddenly he had been thrust into a cold and uncomfortable world. He also was very hungry.

Joseph's wife. Tafiha, smiled up at him and said, "we have a son". Tears rolled down Joseph's cheeks and he fell to his knees to thank his God for this gift of a son. Tafiha cradled the infant in her arms, and began to breast feed him. The child's howls stopped as he eagerly drank his mother's milk. Joseph leaned over and kissed his wife and whispered, "I would like to call him Thomas Joseph", and his wife smiled her agreement.

After spending a short time with his wife and son, Joseph turned to thank the women who had helped his wife to give birth. He turned once again to his family, leaned over to once more kiss his wife and child, and left the house to return to the hills. He knew that his family was in the competent hands of the village women and he also knew that he had best return to the hillside where his Hamid was alone with the flock.

The daily skirmishes with the Druse Muslims were as intense as ever. The problems of the contentious factions that shared the Lebanon hillside went back for centuries and each generation of Christian Lebanese, to which Joseph and his relatives belonged, had to learn to cope with the violence. Although the Christians of Lebanon suffered a great deal because they had a different faith than the Druse of the area, their religion was the foundation of their daily lives. They were devout Christians and every aspect of their lives was based on the tenets of their religion. They attended church faithfully and patterned their daily activities to conform to the church's teachings of living a Christian life.

Joseph, thought of his new indignant son and wondered how he would handle the daily clashes with the Druse. He smiled to himself and vowed that he, Joseph, would teach his son well and raise a strong and forceful man who would be able to handle any strife with which he might be faced.

As Joseph walked back up the hillside of his homeland he reflected upon the history of this ancient land, of the roots of the daily conflict between the Druse and the Christians of the area. This beautiful land, rich in heritage and an historical symbol of the accomplishments of man. This land, that had been subjected to centuries of strife because of man's greed and intolerance of his fellow man. This land, that had been plundered in the name of religion. This land, that had been coveted by many foreign nations and had been shaped by its natives' struggle to be free. This land of 4,034 square miles with its highest peak at Qurnet al-Sawdah, nine thousand feet above sea level. This land, whose mountains had been a refuge for the victims of religious persecution for centuries. And Joseph, a native son of this land, and endowed with an abundance of strength of character, would raise the next generation of native sons to carry on the traditions of this land.

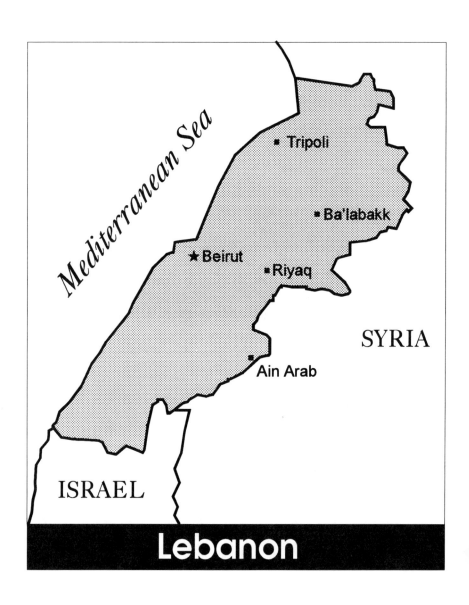

II

The roots of this ancient land that Joseph Assaf El Haddy called home wandered back through the ages of history in much the same way as the ancestors of this land called Lebanon wandered through the geographic area of the world known as the middle east, the orient, and eastern Europe. Just as the shifting sands of the desert through which these ancestral nomads traveled seeking food and shelter erases evidence of man's intrusion upon it, the history of these early ancestors of Lebanon, nomadic tribes known as Bedouins and Giblites, appears and disappears in the annals of history. As does the history of the wandering 'sea people', who joined the nomadic Bedouins and Giblites to become the founding fathers of this land called Lebanon. The Bedouins were known to have migrated from the Sinai and the Giblites, natives of the town of Byblos, were thought to be a mixture of wandering tribes with no particular individuality as a group.

As accurately, but disputably, as historians are able to determine, the history of the Lebanon dates back to the year 332 BC. The meanness of the Sinai desert, from which one of Lebanon's major settler groups came, made survival by man in its midst precarious at best. It gave food and drink to man sparingly and erratically; often filling water wells with its blinding sands driven by the wind, or covering its meager supply of trees with sandstorms, or shriveling them with the burning sun. Those who attempted to live in its midst, such as the Bedouins of the Sinai, soon learned that in order to survive they would have to continually move from location to location in a constant search for the meager needs of life which the desert was unwilling to provide. The deserts' precarious support of life also made it impossible for many newcomers to be added to the ones who were there ahead of them. Consequently, even a few newcomers made it necessary for some of them to move on and hence their nomadic existence. These constant migrations to escape the ravages of the desert brought the

Giblites and the nomads of the Sinai to the fertile crescent of the Mediterranean, which included the Lebanon, and there they were joined by the nomadic 'sea people' who also wandered the earth in search of life's needs.

During the years between 2300 and 2000 BC the great Amurite Migration occurred. The name Amurite is derived from the word Amurru or western land. The migration of these people took them from the mediterranean coast and the desert of the Sinai northward toward Mesopotamia. Some of the members of this migratory band remained behind in the area which was to be called Phoenicia, the area of the Lebanon. They called themselves Canaanites which means lowland peoples or kinabbu, an Akkadian word meaning the red people. Later in history the Greeks would call them Phoinkes, the people from the purple land.

These members of the nomadic migration from the Sinai to the north found that the city of Byblos in the northern part of the Lebanon would provide them with a place where they could live and survive. It was not difficult for these tough sons of the desert at Sinai to overcome the city and make it their own. They had stumbled upon a paradise. Instead of the barrenness of the desert from whence they had come, they found beautiful mountainous country, with snow-capped peaks, mountain streams, large tracts of trees, fertile fields and an area that supported trees that bore figs, olives and other fruits. There was an abundance of game to hunt. The sea was at their doorstep and the climate promised them relief from the burning sun of the desert.

All of these wonderful resources in the Lebanon would shape the future of these nomads for generations to come. When they arrived they were aware that there was a good lumber trade ongoing and in a very short space of time they would take over this trade as their own. Although these migratory Canaanites impacted the town of Bylos because of their sheer numbers, they were in fact just one of the many migrations of nomads that had infiltrated the town. This infusion of people for over a century made the town of Byblos a melting pot of migratory people who had blended together and shaped one another's customs and traditions so that a new and distinct population emerged. The sons of the Sinai would add their individuality to this melting pot and become a major force in its personality. As would the nomadic sons of the sea who had migrated from the north seeking a homeland and had made the waters of the mediterranean their domain.

School house attended by Tom (from 1897-1908)
and Frances (from 1903-1910) Haddy

III

Little Tom rushed through his evening meal as he was very excited at the importance of this night. He had celebrated his fifth birthday two months earlier and had started school early in this month of September of 1897. His teacher was Easa from Rashia Elwadie, a nearby town, and he knew that this teacher was a respected person in his village. But more importantly, he was considered to now be old enough to sit and listen to the elders of his village of Ain Arab as they told the tales of the history of this ancient land called Lebanon. He finished his meal and ran outdoors to impatiently wait for the village elders to gather in the square where the tales would be told.

Tom picked a place for himself near the spot where he knew that the elders would be seated so that he would hear every word that was said. Soon the villagers gathered for the telling of the historic tales. The men of the village, smoking their narghileh pipes, formed a circle. Tom watched as the men filled these Turkish water pipes. As the Persian tobacco burned, the men drew the smoke through cold water in the pipe to lessen the bite of the tobacco on their tongues. And soon the bubbling sound of the water and the aroma of the strong tobacco filled the air. The other townspeople gathered around to listen to the wise old men tell of the history of their land.

Aram the elder was chosen to tell the tale this night and young Kamal, who was sitting nearby asked the old one, "How did our people first come to this land?". And Aram began the tale, "Many centuries ago, on the northern coast of Lebanon there was an area of land that was truly blessed by our creator. This area was cradled between the sea and the mountains, and although the caravans from the south could enter the area, the mountains to the north came down and met the sea and formed a protective barrier for this garden of Eden. Many of our people, during those ancient times, travelled throughout the valleys and hills of Lebanon and beyond, seeking good grazing land for their flocks.

One group of these migrating people came to this place on the coast and called it Byblos. They came in the year 3500 B.C., before the birth of our Lord Jesus. They called themselves Giblites and when they saw what this land had to offer they put down their roots and decided to make this their home. The mountains that lay to the north and the east of them were covered with tall and fragrant smelling trees. Trees that reached to the skies above. It is said that they measured one-hundred and twenty feet high and were approximately twelve feet in width.

The Giblites, who had been travelling in barren areas to the north and south, thought that they had found a paradise. Their gods, who ruled the earth, had heard their plea for a good place to live. The air was cool and comfortable and there was no burning sun to parch their tongues and throats". Rashid, the young goat-herder, who had heard the stories before but knew that Tom was hearing his first tale, asked the old one, "Why was there not enough water where they had come from?", and the old one replied, "The first of our people lived in the deserts where the hot sun, the wind and the sand parched the land, dried up the wells and burned the grasses and trees."

The old man continued his story, "the Giblites began to build their town of Byblos and upon inspection had found that the tall trees of the forest gave off an oil that could be gathered to sell to others. These trees had a flat topped appearance that formed shade for the land below. Our people named them cedar trees and the oil that they gave cedar oil. They also knew that they would be able to build water craft with these tall trees as there were no others available to the south that could compare with them.

The Ancient ones soon had a thriving lumber business with their Egyptian neighbors to the south. They transported the trunks of these large trees to the Egyptian king who wanted them for boats that would help him to build trade in the area. They also sold the thick balmy oil of the trees to the Egyptians who used it to wrap their mummified kings for burial. The Egyptians also wanted the wood of Byblos to put roofs on their houses. As a result of this trade our people became prosperous in their new home.

Twelve centuries later a new wave of migrating people joined them. These Lebanese ancestors were the Bedouin Semites of the Sinai desert to the south. They too had roamed the land in search of grazing land and food and shelter for their families. When the harshness of the Sinai, with is rocks and craggy shores would no longer sustain them they had headed North in the great Amurite migration. History tells us that the biblical Noah's eldest son, Shem, was known as the father of the Semites".

Emile asked the old one, "and how did these new people get along with our early ancestors?", and Aram the elder replied, "each group had the same needs and showed compassion for each other. They joined together to increase their prosperity. The melding of the Giblites and the Semites increased the prosperity of the town of Byblos for a half dozen or more centuries when another infusion of people were added to the Lebanese coastal towns. Between 1700 and 1200 BC there was a huge migration of so-called Aryans who are believed to have come south from the south of Russia and the eastern part of Europe. However, this group of people had as their goal, an invasion of Egypt. This was the third invasion of the great kingdom of Egypt attempted by the Aryans, but it was not to be. Although this horde of would-be invaders were masters of the sea, they controlled the eastern half of the mediterranean and allowed no other ships to ply the waters, they were defeated by Egypt's King Ramses III.

The invaders ocean going ships were becalmed and the smaller and paddle-driven Egyptian craft attacked and destroyed them. The invaders retreated to the safety of the sea and inhabited the many islands of the Mediterranean. This nomadic group from the north decided that the uncertainty of the sea was more to be trusted than the land that they had attempted to invade. They thought that the constantly moving mass of water of the sea was very much like the constantly shifting sands of the deserts that they had travelled and they felt comfortable coping with the sea's uncertainties. They also liked the constant sailing that the sea provided them as it satisfied their restless nature. A restlessness that they thought of as part of their heritage. Thus, they became the "sea people" of ancient times.

They were the best, fastest and bravest seamen of that time and they soon were trading throughout the lands that bordered the waters of the Mediterranean. They soon integrated with the inhabitants of the coastal villages of the Lebanon. As they merged with the Giblites and Semites who had come before them, they brought all of their skills and knowledge with them. They had knowledge of how to extract iron from its ore, by heating the ore to form a liquid and separating the iron from the crude ore. They had learned the secret of how to dye cloth purple by using the excretions of seas snails. By staining cloth with this excretion of the snails and then adding lemon to the stain they discovered that they could dye their cloth to beautiful shades of red and purple.

Because it was difficult to get enough of the excretion from the snails to mass produce this beautiful shade of colored cloth, they made small amounts of the cloth and only sold it to very wealthy customers in the Mediterranean. And because this beautifully colored cloth was so expensive and only available to a few, the color purple came to be known as a sign of wealth, power and influence and these people were then referred to as 'royalty'. Those who wore a purple stripe were of the highest rank or privilege. Because of this making and selling of purple cloth, the Greeks referred to our ancestors as 'Phoinikes' which in the Greek language was taken from the word porphyra which meant purple. But the greatest contribution of these 'sea people' to their new land was their nautical skills. They soon turned the Canaanites from crude rafters of the coastal waters to navigational rulers of the sea."

The young shepherd called Abraham then asked the old elder, "What did this mixture of our ancestors call themselves Umee?" using the respected name of uncle, that all young Lebanese used when talking to their elders. And Aram replied, "this mixture of Giblites, Bedouin Semites and 'sea people' formed a race that would be known as the Phoenicians. And the last group of our ancestors to join the others, the 'sea people', founded villages south of Byblos which they called Tyre and Sidon. All of these happenings forced the Egyptians, who for years had dominated the Lebanon, to release their hold on our ancestors, the Canaanites of Byblos. The coast of the Lebanon, now known as Phoenicia, was to thrive and shape the future of the mediterranean for centuries to come."

Young Karam then asked Aram, "but were these 'sea people' happy when they moved to the land to join the Giblites and the Semites?" and Aram said, "they built their towns as close to the sea as possible. There was a king of the town of Tyre who was named Hiram and he moved his town onto two flat rocky ledges in the sea. These rocks were partly submerged in the water but Hiram built a beautiful castle on the rocks and the Tyrians called this town Sor, which meant rocks in the ancient language of Phoenicia. Hiram believed that they must take refuge in the sea and trust the land as little as possible. Most of the towns that the 'sea people' inhabited were built on pieces of land that jutted into the sea and the rocky coast of the Lebanon. They did this to protect themselves from their enemies and to use the sea as a barrier against those enemies.

Those 'sea people' that made their home in Tyre caused problems for themselves by using the rocks of the shoreline as sites for their towns. There was no water on the rocky land and they could not dig wells in the rock so they depended on rain water but soon found that in the summer time the water that they gathered either evaporated or became polluted. But they were a very resourceful breed and soon learned that there were springs of fresh water at the bottom of the sea water along the coast and by placing a funnel over the naturally bubbling spring and hooking a leather hose to the end of the funnel they could gather sweet and clean water to satisfy their needs. The pressure of the bubbling spring propelled the water to the surface."

The hour was growing late and the elder stopped talking and told the villagers that they had best go home and get some rest as there was work to be done on the morrow. Tom and his family returned to their home for a night's rest but Tom's head was filled with the wonder of what he heard and it was well into the night before he fell asleep.

IV

The next morning Tom awoke early even though he had fallen asleep late the night before. The first thought that entered his mind was the stories that he had heard Aram the elder tell the night before and he knew that he would hear more of these historic tales as it was tradition in his village for the young to be taught the history of their ancestors by listening to the tales of the village elders of the Lebanese people. This tradition of passing on the heritage of the Lebanese people was combined with teaching the children the deep and unfailing Christian faith that these Lebanese villagers had in their God. Going to church and living a Christian life was another of the unshakeable parts of the children's upbringing. The families attended church together in the village and set an example for the children whose beliefs were being molded and nurtured. The fact that the problems that the villagers had with the Druse Muslims was due to their different faith did not deter them from their staunch loyalty to their religion.

Tom arose as he could smell the Turkish coffee that his mother was making. He knew that some of the neighbors would soon be arriving as it was the custom in his village to make early morning visits to one's neighbors in the coolness of the early dawn. These visits were a time for socializing and trading of gossip. Tom felt a warm glow of happiness as he dressed and went to the kitchen where his mother was preparing food for her neighbors. The warmth and love that the villagers felt for each other was evident in their every day life.

As he entered the kitchen Tom saw that his mother had prepared the table with grapes, figs that had been filled with honey, melons and sweet apricots which had been picked from the trees in his father's grove in the backyard. Tom went to the door of the room where his small sister Zarife was sleeping. She was only two years old and would sleep through this early gathering of the neighbors so Tom closed the door to her room and returned to the kitchen. The neighbors soon arrived and Tom felt very grown up and sat at the table so that he could listen to the gossip of the neighbors as they drank the strong coffee and ate the fruits that his mother had prepared.

When they had finished the coffee they inverted their cups in the saucers so that the coffee sediment formed a pattern on the inside of the cup. Then one of the village women acted as the fortune teller and proceeded to 'tell the future' of her neighbors. Everyone laughed as she attempted to give all of them great fortune and good health. Tom giggled at the light-hearted joking of his mother and her friends. They rose to go back to their own homes and the daily work that awaited them. The men who had spent the night in the village, returned to the hills to give the men who had cared for the goats and the sheep during the night a chance to return to the village for food and rest.

Tom and his mother went to the flat surfaced roof of their house to spread the vegetables and fruits that had been picked the day before from their garden. It was getting toward the fall part of the year and they would be preparing foods for storage to be used when the months became cooler and the garden did not produce as much as it did in the hot summer months. They worked steadily, side by side, and Tafiha smiled at the diligence of her young son. He would grow to be a reliable and strong man, she thought. When they were finished they returned to the kitchen below and as Tafiha went to awaken her small daughter and begin to prepare breakfast Tom went to the breek to get a cool drink of water. This narrow-necked, wide-based, earthen jug was kept in the kitchen for drinking water which had been drawn from the village well. The secret of drinking from the jug was to pour the water into ones mouth without touching the jug to ones lips. The jug kept the water cool as it evaporated through the pores of the jug. Tom drank thirstily and then set the jug beside the others that his mother kept for the storing of wines, honey, oils and grains that she used in her kitchen.

An hour later, Joseph, who had spent the night tending the goats on the hillside came home for the family breakfast. A late breakfast for the family was the custom in Tom's village. It was a time for the family to be together and to build the familial bonds that would last a lifetime. Tafiha, had prepared their breakfast of scrambled eggs covered with cuminseed called kamoun, kareeshee or cheese, bread, olives and coffee. Tom and his small sister would drink goat's milk for their breakfast. The family ate heartily and Joseph and Tafiha discussed plans to go to Zahle with other villagers in the next two weeks so that they could take part in the bazaars that were held regularly in that city. Tafiha would take some of her hand made baskets that she had spent the summer making and sell them to the vendors that wandered the streets of the bazaar. They would make it a family holiday and ride to Zahle with other villagers in an ox-cart. Tom was very excited at the prospect of going to the bazaar and turned excitedly to his small sister to tell her of the trip. Zarife giggled at Tom's excitement but did not quite understand why he was so excited. Joseph and Tafiha smiled at their enthusiastic son and Joseph arose to return to the hills.

V

Tom awoke with a start. This was the day that he and his family would go to the bazaar in Zahle and he was afraid that he had slept too long but as he looked out of the window in his bedroom he saw that it was still dark out and he heard his parents preparing for the day trip that they would make. Tom jumped out of bed and went to the kitchen. His parents were preparing the water jugs and a basket of food that they would take with them and use along the way when they or their friends became hungry. They would be leaving soon as the trip was long and they wished to arrive in Zahle early so that they could enjoy a long day at the bazaar. Tafiha folded blankets that she would put in the ox-cart so that Zarife could nap along the way. Tom heard the ox-cart outside at the door and ran out to see who was going with them. Maheeba, his mother's friend and her son Karam who had sat next to Tom in the village square when the historic tales had been told were going, but his father Abdullah would not be going as he would stay with the herd this time and give another man a chance to visit the bazaar. Abraham, the young shepherd and his new wife Freda would also be going with them. Joseph and Tafiha with Zarife bundled in a blanket came out to join their neighbors and all of the supplies for the day were packed in the cart. Abraham would drive the cart to Zahle and he took the driver's seat. When they were all settled he clucked to the oxen who were pulling the cart and they were on their way to a fun-filled day.

The swaying of the cart made Tom drowsy after a while and he put his head down and fell asleep along side of his small sister. The adults talked quietly to each other as they travelled along the road to Zahle. There were many other carts from their village and other villages, as going to the bazaars was a favorite pastime of the people from the small towns of Lebanon and Syria. After several hours they could see the town of Zahle in the distance and the road became crowded with wagons, carts and people riding donkeys. All headed to the bazaar in the streets of Zahle. Tom awoke and became excited as they neared their destination. Abraham and Joseph passed the earthen jug of water to everyone so that they would have their fill of the cool water that they had brought from home. Zarife was hungry so Tafiha gave her some of the fruit and bread that they had with them. Tom ate a small amount too, but he was too excited to eat and stood in the cart so that he could get a better view of the city that they were approaching. Soon they were in the city and Abraham drove the oxen to a nearby pasture behind some of the buildings of Zahle so that they could graze while he, his wife and the El Haddy's visited the bazaar. He released the oxen from the cart and staked them to the ground so that they would not wander away.

The group then walked to the streets where there were many others who would spend the day enjoying themselves. A young boy, several years older than Tom looked at him and shouted, "Halee dirsak ya walad", and Tom smiled as he knew that the young boy was shouting 'food for the sweet tooth, young one'. Tafiha smiled and told Tom they would buy some of the sweets that were being hawked later. Tom looked in awe as he saw many women of the surrounding villages carrying woven baskets, urns and large baskets of bread on their heads. The women would take a spot on the street and set up their wares to sell. Tafiha soon found a buyer for her handmade crafts that she had brought from home and sold them. The buyer would in turn, sell the wares to others who frequented her stall on the corner that she had claimed for herself.

As Tom and his family wandered the streets of the bazaar he eagerly looked, with fascination, at the sights. Men were seated on the ground, hammering chains and necklaces made of gold which were selling as fast as they could make them. There were men seated on the ground on oriental rugs which had been placed before the buildings. They were teaching young Lebanese and Syrians the art of writing graceful Arabic script. They were forming the letters from the right side of the parchment to the left, placing little marks above the letters to indicate the vowels of the words. The streets were filled with stalls and the entire area was ablaze with color. Blankets, clothes, baskets, jugs for kitchen use, and dozens of other items used by the women in running their homes competed for the eyes of the buyers. The men smoked their water pipes as the women bustled about to buy what they could, as they bargained with the vendors, trying to get the best price possible. Children raced through the crowded streets excited by all that was going on. Others of the women and men swirled and danced in the city square to the music of the drums, reed and lutes, whose sounds filled the air. The air was also filled with the smells of the delicious food that was being sold: sweets, cheeses, fruits, vegetables and the traditional dishes of the area; roz, rice dotted with brown orzo; kibby, lamb mixed with wheat, onions and spices which were baked in butter; and batinjam mihshee, eggplant stuffed with lamb and pine nuts. As a young vendor walked past Tom shouting 'Dafee butnak ya birdan '-Warm your stomach, cold one-' Tom began to feel very hungry. His parents and their neighbors who had come to the bazaar with them gathered under a tree and with the food that they had brought with them and some of the delicious food being hawked they had a sumptuous meal. They sat and gossiped with each other for a short time to let their food settle and then resumed their wanderings through the streets of Zahle. As the day began to lengthen and the sun began to tilt toward the west, they piled into the ox-cart and headed back to their village. Tom and his sister were soon asleep in the wagon as the family and their friends headed home after a funfilled day.

It was late when Tom and his family returned to their home and Tafiha put Zarife to bed and told Tom to get some sleep. Tom undressed and climbed into his bed. He was tired from the long day but filled with happiness of the wonderful things that he had seen. As he drifted off to sleep he heard the wail of the lute far up in the hills where the young goatherders were tending the village flocks. It wailed hauntingly over the night air and Tom fell into a deep sleep.

VI

Tom hurried home from school so that he could finish his chores quickly. He was eight years old now and growing very rapidly. He could do many things around the house and his parents gave him an opportunity to learn as much as he could. He hurried to the roof of their home so that he could gather the apricots, figs, dates, olives and spices that had been drying for the past several weeks. His family would have these stored foods for use in the cooler months of the fall and winter and it was now his job to do most of the drying of food for the family. He worked quickly to finish his chores so that after he had his supper he would be ready to go to the village square to hear more tales of the history of his people. He had been to many story-telling gatherings and had never tired of hearing the historic tales of the village elders. As he entered the kitchen his sister Zarife smiled at him and showed him a picture that she had been making. Tom smiled at his younger sister and praised her efforts. He remembered when he was five and had so eagerly tried to learn all that was around him. He understood how important it was for Zarife to learn and grow as he had. He now had a little baby brother too. His name was George and he had been born last year and was now one year old. His mother was finishing the preparations of their supper and the fragrant smells made Tom's mouth water.

It was September and Tom's family were to have a traditional September meal made up of stuffed squash, fried kibby, lamb and a salad. He had watched his mother and had often helped her in preparing the wheat that she used to make their kibby. He had learned the steps used to prepare the wheat for use. After it was harvested, the wheat was washed in the river nearby, and laid in the sun to dry out. Then his mother, like the other village women, had put the wheat in a large pot and had cooked it for hours. The cooked wheat was then laid in the sun to dry once more. The wheat was then sorted, the chaff being separated from the wheat. His mother had then taken the wheat to the stone mill to be ground and the processed wheat had then been stored for use.

Tafiha had prepared the kibby for their supper in the traditional manner. She had taken the ground lamb and mixed it with onions, cracked wheat, spices and water. She then kneaded this mixture, adding water as she kneaded. She then simmered lamb in butter, adding salt, pepper and pine nuts which had been browned in butter. She then prepared the mixtures for baking by layering the two mixtures in a pan. She had prepared the stuffing for the squash earlier by mixing chopped lamb, rice, pureed tomatoes, butter and spices. After scooping out the core of the squash she had filled it with the filling mixture, sprinkled dried mint over the top and had baked it with the kibby. She prepared a salad of fresh vegetables and olives and brewed a pot of coffee. Joseph would join them for this evening meal as it was his turn to have a night off from tending the herd on the hillside. She prepared fruits and cheese for their dessert and Tom helped his mother to finish preparing the table as his father arrived home.

After finishing their meal the El Haddys went to the village square to join their fellow villagers to hear the tales told by the village elders of the ancient history of their land. When everyone was seated and the men had filled their pipes for the evening smoke, Bisharra, the eighty-five year old townsman, who still went to the hills to help care for the goat herds, was asked to tell the historical tales for the evening.

Bisharra began, "Our ancestors thrived in the town on the coast of the Lebanon that they called Byblos. They, along with the southern coastal towns of Tyre and Sidon, traded the wood from the tall cedar trees on the mountain called Hermon; they traded papyrus, earthenware, food, cloth, tin, iron, lead, silver, brass, emeralds, embroidered goods, linens, coral, agate, medicines, spices, and dyes". "But Umee", said Emile, who was approaching his manhood, "did our ancestors have all of the things necessary to make the goods that they traded?" and Bisharra replied, "no, but that is why our ancestors were so very successful. They looked to see what raw materials they had on their own land that could be used for profitable trades. They found that the sands on their shores contained quartz which could be used for making glass. The Egyptians had known of the process of making glass in the fourth century and our ancestors took that skill and developed it for profitable trade. They mixed quartz with ash from the salt in the sea and then they added an alkali, heated it and found that they could make beads and blow the mixture into glass objects. They started their own glass manufacturing industry. They made the first transparent glass in history. They discovered the technique of glass blowing.

Our ancestors were artisans who produced trinkets from imported ivory, made vessels of bronze, made vases of clay and glazed them, they made necklaces, bracelets and items for the general use of all of their customers. They were a small country but prided themselves on making small but needed items that brought them great profits". Bisharra continued, "Tyre and Sidon were at a disadvantage to Byblos in wood trading because they had to transport the wood from a distance. And all three towns, Byblos, Tyre and Sidon were targets for raiders from the sea but they protected themselves from the would be invaders. All of the papyrus of that time was made in Egypt but was shipped to Greece from our ancients' town of Byblos, which is the Greek word for papyrus.

Our ancestors also dealt with the sifting sands of the sea beds which became choked with silt. They built a system of tidal basins and canals. The winds drove clean surface water into the inner harbor. The pressure from this wind-driven water forced the muddied water underneath to be driven down and to be forced out to sea through the channels that they had built. And the harbor was cleansed.

These ancient 'sea people', Bedouins and Giblites were considered to be the best seaman and sea merchants. They were shrewder than their neighbors, thought in a practical manner and were more technically adept. The harshness and the constant uncertainty of their early existence had forced them to develop their mental and physical powers. They could only survive by using their wits and mental powers. They had learned a great deal from all with whom they came in contact; for instance, from the Egyptians they learned about pyramid building and the mathematics that was used in building pyramids. They also honed their skills in their daily dealings with the sea which continually provided them with new challenges.

The ' sea people' who joined our early ancestors and became united with them taught the people who lived in the Lebanon how to build ships for trade and protection when on the sea. One type of boat that they built was long and narrow. It had two rows of oars, was very fast in the water and the oarsmen could hang their shields over the side of the boat. It had a small sail and was easy to manipulate in the water. Our ancestors used this boat to fight off the pirates in the area who tried to rob them when they were at sea. The second type of boat that the ancients built was short and wide but needed fewer oarsmen and had a large square sail. This boat had a large hold and high rails on the deck so that our ancestors could carry a great deal of merchandise on their trading trips. The one thing that they had to worry about with this boat was that it could be swamped easily. And the third type that they built was a cross between the other two. It needed more oarsmen than the short boat, could be used to transport goods but was armed and used to fight off their enemies.

The 'sea people' brought with them a knowledge of building keeled ships and our ancestors soon saw the advantage of building ships in this way. They realized that these boats did not pitch when hit with a swell of the sea, were easier to maneuver and were much steadier in the water. They also learned that if the boat had holes to hold the oars and the oarsmen sat with their backs to the front of the ship it would go much faster and steadier. The length of the keels of these boats was limited by the length of the tallest cedar tree that they could find. The captains of the 'sea people' sailed by the sun, the moon and the stars. None of the other seamen in the area could match their nautical skills. They used short coastal routes throughout the Mediterranean and hopped from island to island for nautical safety and to confuse the pirates looking for them.

"Bisharra", said Joseph, "tell our young ones how we know of these ships that our ancient ancestors used", and Bisharra continued the tale. "We know of these boats because pictures of their ships were carved on the walls of their tombs. The boats had deep bellies and high rails on the deck. They used webbing on the upper part of the mast to raise and hold the spars. These were the ones that swamped the most often.

Our ancestors also developed an alphabet that they had seen used by some early semitic tribe. Our ancestors fully developed this system into an alphabet, which was superior to what the Greeks were using at that time. Our merchant seamen taught it to the Greeks with whom they came in contact during their travels and the Greeks took that alphabet as their own. Later in history they would teach it to the Romans who then taught it to the world.

The land of our ancestors, known as Phoenicia then, began to grow as a trading country. As the towns of Tyre and Sidon grew so did the prosperity of all of our people. They had started by trading wood with the

Egyptians, who had always treated our ancestors as serfs, to expanding their trading empire and becoming the leaders in wholesale trade in the Mediterranean. They conducted their business by going to all of the small towns that dotted the Mediterranean shores where they would spread their wares on the beaches on blankets. They wanted to build a fair trade with their customers based on honesty and mutual respect so that after they had spread their wares, they would build a huge fire on the shore and the smoke would let the villagers know that the traders were there. Our ancestors would then return to their ships and wait for the villagers to inspect the wares and offer a price in gold for them. When the villagers had made an offer of gold they would retreat and the merchant seamen would come to the shore to see what had been offered. If they did not think that the money offered was sufficient they would return to the ship and wait for the villagers to offer a better price. When the gold offered was suitable to the ancients they gathered up the gold and returned to their homeland. Neither the villagers nor the merchants would touch what belonged to the other until both sides were satisfied with the sale. In this way our ancestors built a trade with all of the villages based on respect and trust. Both sides wished for the transactions to continue as the sea merchants did not want to lose their customers and the villagers wanted the sea merchants to bring their goods to their villages.

As time went on the ancients started to substitute expensive products made of wood instead of transporting the lumber to the towns and countries with which they traded. They found this more profitable than the wood sales as transporting the wood was clumsy and time consuming. Our ancestors realized that if they took raw materials from the town in barter for their goods, they could then take the raw materials home, fashion it into something beautiful or useful and sell it back to the villagers for a huge profit. They also realized that products made from materials in their own land would bring even greater profits. So they founded their own industries and workshops"

"Tell the young ones of the king of Tyre who built a castle on the sea", said Abraham, who was sitting next to Tom. And Bisharra told the tale. "In the year 1000 BC, there was a King named Hiram who moved his town from the coast of Lebanon out into the sea. The town was built on two flat rocky ledges that were partly submerged in the water. Here, Hiram built a castle and his town was considered one of the most beautiful of ancient times. This town of Tyre was also known as 'Sor', a word that meant rocks to the ancient ones. As you know, our ancestors did not trust the land and sought safety by living as close to the sea as possible".

The hour was growing late and Bisharra bade his neighbors 'good night' as the men put out their pipes and the villagers returned home for a night's rest. The next day was Sunday and the villagers and their families would go to church to worship and observe the Sabbath as good Christians were expected to do.

VII

The years were passing swiftly and Tom was now twelve years old. It was the spring of the year and Joseph was preparing to drive the goats, along with those of his fellow villagers back to Ain Arab. He and the other men drove their herds to the grazing lands south of Ain Arab each winter as the grazing on their own hillside was sparse at this time of the year. There were 1200 head in the combined herd of the villagers. It had taken them five days to herd the goats to this grazing area and it was getting toward the spring of the year. It was time to return to their village before the Easter season. Joseph, as the leader of the group called together all of the men and they gathered the goats into a combined herd for the trip back. After the first day on the road back it began to rain and as the rain fell heavily the men and animals began to tire from the harshness of the weather. Tom was having a hard time keeping his eyes open, but as this was the first time that his father had allowed him to go with the men on the long trek Tom did not want his father to think that he could not keep up with the others so he fought to stay awake. Soon, they heard the heavy hoofbeats of the horses descending upon them. The Druse attacked Tom's Uncle John and were trying to beat him on the head with heavy clubs. Joseph ran to the leader of the group and pulled the man from his horse as the man tried to hit him with his club. Soon there was fierce fighting between the two groups. The rain poured down and Tom looked on miserably and wondered why there was such bad blood between his people and these people called the Druse. Soon the villagers drove off the attackers and the Druse remounted their horses and galloped away. "Why do they hate us so, father?", asked Tom.

And Joseph replied, "Many years ago in the year 985 there was a man who was called the Fatimid Caliph of Egypt, a follower of the Muslim faith. His name was Al-Hakim and he declared himself the incarnation of God. He had two assistants who decided the beliefs of his followers. Their names were Hamza and Darazi. Darazi went to Lebanon from Egypt to preach his interpretation of the Muslim faith. His followers were called the Druse. In the year 1840 our land was ruled by the Ottoman Empire of Turkey and the Sultan of Turkey sent his princes to rule our land. Under these princes, the first was called Bashir III and the second one was called Omar Pasha, our people were made to pay unfair taxes and bitter fighting started between the Druse and our Christian ancestors. In Turkey the Sultan asked for advice from the European countries on how to stop the fighting between the Druse and the Christians and the European countries suggested to the Sultan that our land be divided between the Christians and the Druse. The Sultan agreed and in 1842, under a Turk named Assa'd Pasha our country was divided. There was a northern district for our Christian people and a southern district for the Druse. The road between Damascus and Beirut was the dividing line between the districts. Bitter fighting started once again as other countries interfered in how our people would live.

The French supported our people and the British supported the Druse. These outside influences turned a disagreement over the use of the land and unfair taxation between the two groups of Lebanese people into a bitter religious feud. In 1860 the Druse killed thirty thousand of our Christian people. The bitterness is still with us and them." Tom was silent as he listened to his father's words. The band of goatherders quietly finished their trip home and Tom was glad to see his warm and secure house.

After several days of rest the villagers returned to their normal routines of living. The Easter season was upon them and this was a most holy season for the Lebanese Christians. Tom had joined the other children of his village and had helped to gather pomegranate skins and vegetable roots for the coloring of the Easter eggs which was part of the Easter celebration. His people called them Bythet il eed. Tafiha had spent many days preparing the pastries and breads for her family and her friends. She had made Tom's favorite sweet, baklava. She had made pastry sheets using the traditional Lebanese recipe of flour, olive oil, salt, egg whites and warm water. She had mixed the ingredients, kneaded the dough that was formed and had let it set in a warm place as the recipe required. Then she had cut the dough in sections and had dipped the pieces in cornstarch. Again the dough was allowed to set and then the dough was rolled into very thin sheets which were then cut into strips to fit the baking pan. These were covered with thin paper and were then ready for the making of the favorite sweet of the village children. Tafiha had layered her pan with the paper thin pastry sheets and had brushed each sheet with butter and then added the next pastry sheet to the pan and had continued to butter each sheet as it was added. She had then slowly baked the pan filled with buttered pastry sheets until the tops were a golden brown. She had then made the syrup that was traditionally poured over the baked pastry sheets mixing honey, sugar and lemon and boiling this mixture which when cool would be poured over the cooked pastry sheets.

Tom looked forward to these special seasons of his people and the delicious food that was served. He liked the elegance of the table that his mother set for these special occasions and the beautiful damask tablecloths that she used as these heirloom cloths were made and handed down from generation to generation of Lebanese wives. His mother's cooking like that of all of the other Lebanese women of his village was like the people, imaginative, colorful and exotic with the delicate use of herbs and spices. The food was arranged artistically and designed to tempt the ones who would eat it. It did.

The Springtime was especially beautiful in his homeland and Tom looked forward to this time of the year as it was a busy time of planting their garden and tending the fruit trees which gave them the delicious fruits that they enjoyed fresh and dried for winter use. He finished his chores and washed his hands and face, for after dinner this evening the villagers would gather once more for the telling of more historic tales. His younger sister Zarife and his small brother George were also listening to the tales of the village elders so that they too could learn of the honorable heritage of their ancestors.

Selim, who was approaching the age of eighty, would relate the historic tales tonight. The villagers gathered and he began.

"The ancients controlled the trade routes of the Mediterranean for centuries. They heard that silver could be gotten further west and as they were now more interested in raw materials that they could make into merchandise that could bring them a good profit they established a trade route from Tyre to Utica to Cadizz and were soon trading along the coast of Spain. Their superior nautical skills made it easy for them to establish new trade routes. They soon learned if they sailed along the coast of North Africa during the summer months of the year they would run into violent storms so that they sailed along the coast of southern Europe, crossed over to Spain and used the route along the North African shore on their journey home. Using these routes they always had favorable winds for their sailing. They were very secretive on why they took these routes so that they would not have many competitors and they told wild stories of shipwrecks and sea monsters to further discourage their competition. They not only got silver from Spain but brought home tin for use in many articles to trade. The ancients said that the tin was brought to the Spanish coast by the 'tin islands' but our ancestors later thought that these islands were really the islands of Great Britain. Our ancestors could now fuse tin with copper to get bronze.

Our ancestors prospered and grew and were soon trading and doing business with countries and towns in all of the area. When King David, the founder of Israel, built his army and defeated the Philistines of biblical times, Hiram, the King of Tyre, looked upon David's victories as an opportunity to expand the influence and wealth of his people. To encourage David to turn to Tyre for his needs the king sent him cedar trees, and some of his best skilled workers, carpenters and stonemasons, as he realized that David would have to build an elaborate residence as a newly established power. David felt that he should build a temple for his new kingdom and other buildings in keeping with the importance that he wished for his people but as he did not have any craftsmen available he hired the Tyrians to do his building. But David would not live to see his planned buildings finished; he died and his son Solomon was left to finish the task. Solomon wrote to Hiram and asked that the temple that they were working on when David died be finished. Hiram agreed and asked that Solomon repay him by giving Tyre thousands of tons of wheat and liters of oil in payment for the years that his craftsmen worked in Israel.

Hiram's men then set themselves up as supervisors and architectural planners of the temple and the Hebrews worked as laborers to complete the temple. Our ancestors supervised and built the public buildings for Israel. The buildings and residences surrounded a large courtyard and the pillars, made of gold and emeralds, stretched skyward and shone in the darkness of night. The buildings were ornate and of the most lavish of the times. Our ancestors built a complex, using Egyptians architectural design, with holy rooms for prayer and religious meetings that served as the center of the religious life of the inhabitants of the town. Our ancestors did extremely careful and precise work and were known throughout the area as the best craftsmen available. The inside walls of the temple were covered with cedar wood and the cloth curtains within were dyed blue and purple by our ancestors.

The cost in wheat and oil that the subjects of King Solomon paid was very high for such a small country and the taxes that the king asked his people to pay were so high that his kingdom was near bankruptcy, so Hiram offered to forget some of the debt that the King of Israel owed in exchange for getting copper from King Solomon's mines. The ancients then made many useful items from this copper and sold it throughout their trade routes and by having this partnership with the King of Israel our ancestors also gained new trade routes to the East African and Indian shores. The King of Israel prospered when our ancestors used his copper and our people also prospered with the extended trade that developed. So both sides profited from the relationship."

Then Emile asked Selim to tell of the history of their lands when Alexander the Great had invaded their lands and Salim looked sad and once again began, "The great military leader of Macedonia had been at war with the Persians and had defeated them. He decided to next march down the one-hundred and thirty miles of the lubnan", said Selim, using the arabic name for Lebanon, "and would then be in a position to attack Egypt. Alexander thought that he had better convince his army generals that this should be done before he attempted to do so. He told his men that he had been told in a dream that the towns along the Lebanon coast that were built in the sea really belonged to the mainland. Especially the fortress town of Tyre. When leaders of those times tried to get their subjects to do something that they wanted they often said that decisions were revealed to them in dreams so that if they proved to be wrong, they could blame it on misinterpretation of a dream and not lose face with their people.

The ancients were highly respected by most of the people of the Mediterranean area at that time for their skills, both as seamen and as makers of goods that they sold for the riches that they possessed. Alexander, realized that his trip down the coast of our land might not be agreed to by our ancestors so he sent representatives to each of the coastal towns and requested that his army be allowed to march through the area. Most of the small towns agreed but when his messenger got to Tyre they were surprised to be told that Alexander's request to pay tribute to their God Melquart was turned down. The Tyrian king, Hiram, did offer to build an altar outside the city where Alexander could pay tribute to Tyre's God. Alexander was furious with this insult to his request so he decided that the way to beat the Tyrians was to build a causeway to their city and he felt that once Tyre was not protected by water around them his army could defeat them in battle. Sadly, he was right. His men built the causeway to Tyre and then attacked our ancestors and destroyed the town of Tyre. To show the world that he defeated our ancestors, Alexander crucified two thousand men of our ancestors and sold thirty-thousand women, children and old people as slaves." Salim stopped talking and the villagers sat quietly as they listened to the sad tale. Some of the villagers openly wept. The men put out their pipes and the villagers quietly walked to their homes.

VIII

Tom sat on the ground with his back against a tree as he watched over his father's herd of goats on the hillside. His dog and the shotgun that he carried for protection of the herd were close by. He had just celebrated his eighteenth birthday several weeks before and he was deep in thought. It was a beautiful clear summer day. His mind wandered to the previous years of his boyhood and the experiences that he had while helping his father to care for the goat herd. He remembered starting school at the age of five and the warm and happy home that his parents had provided for him in his growing years. He remembered the pride that he had felt when his father had allowed him to leave school at the age of sixteen and he had taken on the responsibilities of manhood by being treated as an equal with the other men on the hillside who were earning their living and caring for their families just as his father did. He remembered his mother telling him that he had been baptized by a Father Toomahind into the Christian faith at the age of two months.

He remembered the first time when, at the age of eight, his father had allowed him to travel with the village men as they drove their flock to more fertile grazing to the south as they did every year in the winter season. Tom had felt quite grown up as the oldest son. Now he had a second brother who had been born two years earlier in 1908 and his name was Nicola. He remembered how proud he had felt when he realized that his father was looked upon as the leader of the group because he was fearless and wise and the other men looked to him to bring them and their flocks safely through the trip. Tom remembered that on that trip he had his first experience with the violence that occurred when the Druse and the Christians clashed over grazing land. He remembered the night when the men had been attacked on the way home from the southern grazing land and how his father had explained the bad feelings between the Druse and his people.

He remembered the horror that he had felt when at the age of twelve the Druse had attacked once more when he and his father and Uncles, John and Mike, were tending the goats on the hillside. The thunder of the horses hooves as the Druse bore down on them had filled him with terror. They had once more attacked Uncle John because he had a shotgun that they wanted. Uncle John had refused to give the gun to his attackers. Again Joseph had come running from the village where other herdsmen had shouted down to him about the attack. When Joseph arrived on the scene several villagers and several more Druse had entered the fray. Tom remembered how his father had talked to one of the horsemen who was pretending to be a lawman and had warned him to take his fellow Druse and leave the hillside. The Druse had retreated and Tom thought that at that moment his father, with his strength and wisdom had averted a bloody battle between the Druse and the Christians.

He remembered that since he had been on this hillside he himself had been in several clashes with the hated Druse. He looked down to his right arm, at the elbow that had been broken when he had put his arm up to shield himself from the blows of the Druse on horseback who had attacked him while he tended his father's herd. The elbow, that had not healed properly, and would be forever in the locked position that it was in, would never allow him to raise that arm and use that elbow normally again. He remembered how his father had once asked him to take care of the goats as he wanted to till a patch of land for a garden and Tom had argued that he would prefer to till the land and his father had patiently explained to him the honor of work, any type of work, and Tom had tended the goats. As his mind reflected on the years of his childhood and young manhood he grew troubled as he knew that the rest of his life would be more of the same that he had experienced and although he had grown to be a tall strong man he realized that he wanted more of life than this gave him. He thought of his uncles, John and Mike who had left Ain Arab to find their future in a land called America, miles across the sea.

He realized that he was now eighteen years of age and he could expect that he would soon be taken into the army of the Turkish Sultan, as the Sultan required that young Lebanese and Syrian men join his Army when they became of age. For this was how the Sultan filled the ranks of his military so that the young Turks would not have to serve and run the risk of being killed in their young manhood. The thought of having to spend the best years of his life as a soldier for a foreign country depressed Tom.

As he was lost in his thoughts his mind wandered and he did not hear the thunder of the hoofbeats as they once again descended upon him. Two grown men on horseback rode up and began to beat him on his head with their clubs. Tom had no choice but to once again fend off his attackers. He pulled one of the men from his horse and the other jumped to the ground. They fought furiously and as they fought Tom stumbled backwards and his foot became wedged between two rocks. He continued to fend off his attackers and other herdsmen who were on the hill began to shout for the villagers. The men remounted their horses to get away and Tom grabbed the shotgun that he had with him and began to shoot at them. Because his foot kept him trapped he could not get a good shot off and the men escaped. Blood poured from Tom's head and foot. He was overwhelmed with frustration as he gathered his herd and headed toward the town. As he struggled to herd the goats toward the village his mind raced furiously and the foremost thought in his mind was that he could no longer think in terms of his future here in the midst of the violence and hatred that the Druse Muslims inflicted upon him and his people. Other herdsmen who had witnessed Tom's fight with the horsemen had run to the village to tell Joseph of Tom's plight so that as Tom approached the village with the herd his father and mother came running toward him.

His mother began to cry as she attempted to stop the bleeding and Joseph began to angrily shout at his son in frustration. Tom looked at his father and said, "Father I can no longer stand to care for the goats and to fight the Druse. Please let me go to America to join my uncles, John and Mike, to seek my future. The Druse are impossible to deal with rationally and although there is plenty of grazing land for their goats and ours they hate us, call us filthy names, beat us, and hate our religion. Please let me go to America. I cannot go back to the hills tomorrow to tend the goats." Joseph looked sadly at his tall and earnest son and Tafiha fell to her knees sobbing uncontrollably. She begged Tom not to speak of leaving them and as Tom saw how upset his mother was he fell silent. Tom returned to his home where his mother bound his wounds and prepared him some food.

Several days later Joseph came down from the hillside where he had been thinking of his son's request to go to America to join his uncles. For the past several days he had talked to his son and tried to convince him that he could cope with the Druse and should remain in Lebanon but Tom had been adamant about leaving. Joseph had remembered when he too, several years before Tom's birth had gone to America to try to establish himself but had been forced to return to Lebanon when he had received word that his beloved wife had been accidently shot and wounded. He had hurriedly returned to Lebanon and had decided that he would build a life for himself and his family in his homeland. He understood Tom's frustration and desire to seek a better future than that afforded him in Ain Arab. He approached his son and embraced him. He then said, "I have tried to convince you that you must remain here with your family, but I do not think that I can convince you so you have my permission to go to America and I will give you the money for your passage." Tom was overjoyed at his father's decision. He had packed his belongings earlier in the hopes that his father would agree to let him go. He was only waiting to hear his father give him his blessings and say that he would give him the passage money to America.

After several days of hasty preparation Tom was ready to join the fifteen other villagers who had been making plans to travel to America and Tom would be making the trip to America with them. His mother was quiet and unhappy but said nothing to Tom as she realized that all of her pleading would not change his mind on making the trip across the sea. She quietly helped him to gather his clothes together and helped to prepare himself for his trip.

On the morning that he was to leave Tom arose very early and put his belongings into a carrying case and waited for the rest of the family to arise. Soon after his parents and his brothers and sister arose and dressed to see him off, Tom and his family went to the their church and prayed for Tom's safety on the long journey that he was about to take. They then returned home and had breakfast together for the last time before Tom's departure. After breakfast his mother and father walked with him toward the flour mill in the village where he would meet the other travelers and where the group would start the journey to Beirut harbor to board the steamer that would carry them to America. As they walked his father talked quietly to Tom as he said, "You are starting on a trip that will take you many miles from us. Once you leave you will be alone to face the world. If you find good and honorable people with which to associate you will be a good and honest man. If you work hard and live a clean life and only associate with decent people you will have a good life. If you make oar and spend one dollar and one penny you will be broke, but if you make one dollar and only spend ninety-nine cents then you will have saved a penny, and if you continue to do this you will in a short time have money saved and you will never be broke. You must always be honest in your dealings with other people and you must always treat other people with respect. If you live this way other people will respect you and you will be able to make your way in the world. Always remember that the family is the most important thing in your life. If you raise a family that works and stays together you will have a strong and good family. A family is like a bunch of sticks that are tied together, it is very hard to break them apart, but if the members of the family are separated, it is very easy for outsiders to attack and the strength of the family is weakened. Look at my fist, if I double up my fist it is very strong, but if I open my hand and spread my fingers you can see that the fingers are not as strong apart as they are together. That is the same way as with a family. You are leaving home but you have relatives in America and they are your family too. I expect you to respect your uncles as you have been taught to respect me." As they approached the flour mill Tom's mother fainted and Tom and his father put cool water on her to arouse her. When she was revived, she grasped Tom about his knees and once again begged him not to leave. Tom was saddened at his mother's misery but told her that he must go to America to seek his future. As Tom moved away from his parents they sat on a rock and Tom continued to walk down the road to meet the other travelers. After he had walked several hundred feet Tom turned to look back at his parents.

His mother was sitting with her head on her arms and Tom knew that she was weeping. His father sat on a rock with his head in his hands and Tom knew that he too was weeping. As he looked at his father Tom realized that his father was probably thinking that he would never see his son again. Tom would learn that his father's fears were well founded. In 1911 Tom's mother would give Tom another brother named Elias and in 1913 he would have another sister named Faride and it would be many, many years before he saw them.

His parents sat on the rock and watched as Tom disappeared from view. Tom resolutely kept his eyes looking ahead so that he would not have to look at his weeping parents and finally he met up with the other fourteen Ain Arab villagers who would travel with him to America.

In making the decision to go to America, Tom would be the next in a long line of El Haddys to emigrate to this land far away that promised a better life for all. He was saddened that he would be leaving his father and mother, his sister Zarife, his brother George and his brother Nicola, who was just two years old, but his trip would make him a part of the history of the El Haddy family.

About one hundred and fifty years earlier a man named George El Haddy, Tom's great-grandfather lived in Ain Arab, Syria, which was to become Ain Arab, Lebanon. This man had four sons, Eide El Haddy, Assif El Haddy, Hallil El Haddy and Abusumra El Haddy. These four sons had the following children who emigrated to the United States of America. In 1892 George Eide El Haddy and his two sisters Dihne and Marriam were the first to go to the new land. In 1895 Salem and his brother Mike Abusumra El Haddy followed. Also in 1895 David and his two brothers, Slaman and George El Haddy went to the new land. Then Joseph and his brother Mike Assaf El Haddy followed in 1896. Elias and his brother Hanna Eide El Haddy also made the trip in 1896. Sadie Abusumra El Haddy emigrated in 1904 and Sam Abusumra El Haddy emigrated in 1905. John George Eide El Haddy also went to America in 1905. John Assaf El Haddy made the trip in 1907. And Tom would be the next in line to go to America in this year of 1910.

IX

The group from Ain Arab started their journey by walking together and after several miles were met by a farmer who offered them the use of his donkeys. Some of the women climbed onto the donkeys and the men continued to walk. At six o'clock in the evening they reached the town of Shtarau where George David, their leader had made arrangements for the group to board a train which was to take them to Beirut. They arrived in Beirut the next morning and as Tom descended from the train he gazed to the west and for the first time in his life saw the ocean. He looked in amazement at the vast body of water. George David hurried the group into hiding as there were several young men in the group and any young man caught trying to leave the country would have been immediately arrested and accused of trying to avoid being drafted into the army of the Turkish Sultan. At that period in time the Turkish government dominated the area and the young Lebanese Christian and Syrian men lived in fear of being forced into military service by the Sultan's men. While Tom and his group remained in hiding they were joined by another fifteen Lebanese who would also travel with them to America. As darkness fell, the group were brought to a small boat lying in the harbor. This small boat would deliver them to their ship anchored in the harbor. The small boat pitched and bucked on the choppy harbor water and Tom, who had never been on a boat before suddenly wished that his father were there as he knew, at that moment, that he would have returned to Ain Arab. The small boat made its way toward the ship in pitch blackness and as they approached the ship Tom thought that it looked like a large mountain, but a mountain that was moving up and down with the sea.

The travelers were instructed to climb the rope ladder that hung over the side of the boat, and slowly they each climbed the ladder to the ship's deck. Once they were all aboard the crew instructed them to go below deck to the steerage part of the ship. The captain did not want to have them seen by anyone on shore and risk having the Sultan's men attempt to stop the ship's leaving the harbor. Tom had a small folding chair with him that he had bought in Beirut and on the first night at sea he slept in the chair and cried himself to sleep. The next day, although the harbor was choppy and the winds blew, the ship hoisted its anchor and headed out through the Mediterranean sea. Tom was seasick the entire day but once the first twenty-four hours had passed his seasickness left him and he felt better.

He went to the upper deck to see what the sea looked like when one was traveling on it and again was awed by its vastness. He began to realize that he had embarked on a trip to a land far away about which he knew nothing. He began to talk to his companions to ease the loneliness that he was feeling and one, a twelve year old girl named Fedwa Shaheen, whose first name would be changed to Francis when she got to America, was traveling with her brother Tom and other companions talked to him. She was going to America to join her parents who had left for the new land earlier and had sent for her and her brother to join them.

After several days, as the ship had passed through the Mediterranean, past the boot of Italy, past the North African shore and was entering the harbor at Marseille, France, Tom began to feel excitement at the new and different lands that he would see on his journey and as he descended from the ship he looked around him to take in the sights of this new land that he had never seen. The group was herded into a large room where they would be checked for any diseases which would stop them from traveling to America. Most of the people were sound but the wife of George David their leader was pregnant and her body was covered with a rash. The emigration officials informed Mr. David that his wife could not travel to New York until her condition was cleared up. George David made arrangements for his wife to return to Ain Arab and then met with the group of travelers and suggested that they take a different route to America through the Caribbean. Although they knew that they were supposed to be going to a place called Ellis Island in America, none of the travelers knew of any other way to handle this setback so they agreed to go the suggested route. These problems caused the group to be delayed for ten days in Marseille but finally Mr. David was able to put the group on a train to Cherborg where they would meet the ship which would take them to America. As they departed from the train in Cherborg they were herded into a large building where they would once again be examined by the immigration department of the United States of America.

As they walked down a long narrow corridor, Tom and one of his companions realized that they were carrying a bottle of liqueur and wondered if the officials would object. Tom asked one of the young women travelling with them if she would hide the bottle in her clothing thinking that no one would search her. As they walked down the corridor the bottle dropped from the girl's clothing and broke on the cement floor. Tom hurried to her side, took her arm and told her to keep walking and to pretend that the bottle was not hers. The girl did so and because the crowd was so dense in the corridor no one noticed the broken bottle.

The group was approved to travel to America and Mr. David herded them to the harbor where they would board their ship. The ship carried cargo to Central America as well as the peasant immigrants in its hold. As they boarded the ship they were instructed to go below where there was a large room that they would share with many other passengers. The room was filled with people and soon became hot and uncomfortable but Tom thought that he would soon be on his way and in no time would reach his destination. He did not know that it would be months before he would see his relatives in the new world. As the ship cleared the harbor and headed into the Atlantic the immigrants stood on the deck and watched the French coast disappear from view. As the shoreline receded Tom looked at the water that surrounded him and felt uneasy when he realized that this ship was alone on the high seas and was the only thing that stood between him and a watery grave.

As the days passed the two hundred immigrants that were crowded in the hold of the ship became friends and shared their hopes and their fears for their new lives in this place called America. They were fed subpar food, often no more than soup made from pigs feet. There were no lavatory facilities and they were forced to use the ocean to discard their human waste. They shared the limited water that they had for drinking and used seawater when trying to keep themselves clean. The crew took advantage of the immigrants and overcharged them for the slightest convenience. Tom was a friendly and handsome young man and he soon learned that he could visit the first class section of the ship if the crew were not looking. He went often to this section of the ship and the people there gave him some of their food which was of a much better quality and quantity than that being given to the immigrants traveling in the hold of the ship.

After ten days at sea as they were headed down the coast of Africa on their way to St. Thomas, in the Caribbean, the ship was hit by a major storm. The storm hit suddenly and none of the immigrants in the hold thought it would last long or be severe so they gathered together and consoled one another that the storm would soon be over and they could go up on deck for some fresh air. None had ever before experienced a major storm at sea. The ship, an ocean-going tramp steamer, coal burning, dirty but sea worthy, had seemed so large to the travelers when they boarded her in Cherborg but suddenly it seemed like a cork on the vast sea. The rain began to cascade down in torrents and soon engulfed the ship. At times the water on deck was two feet high. The ship rolled and bucked against the pounding waves, some as high as a two story house.

The waves smashed down on the ship as it fought to remain afloat. Spray from the foam of the water broke over its bow as it plowed through the wind and waves. The fury of the storm intensified as the high winds screamed through the ships cables. The winds increased to gale force and drove the water that lashed at the ship in a frenzy. The thunder crashed from above and the jagged streaks of lightning lit up the deck in an eerie and frightening glow. The ship continued to pitch and buck on the waves and rode it like a roller coaster. Its aft rose into the air with its propeller wildly spinning and seeking the water level so that it could propel the ship forward. The ship increasingly became a victim of the fury of the sea. Its metal plates screamed shrilly, it creaked and groaned from the pounding that it was being subjected to. It rattled and shook and seemed to the frightened passengers to be about to break apart. The waves increased in height and seemed to reach to the sky. The angry sea continued to batter this man made intrusion in an attempt to erase her from its midst.

Below in the bowels of the ship the immigrants were being buffeted with each succeeding crash of the waves. They were tossed about like puppets and soon all were ill. No one was allowed on deck. There was no fresh air in the hold and no toilet facilities. The air in the room in which they were huddled soon became foul with sweat, vomit and excrement of the masses. The bunk beds which were attached to poles that went from the floor to the ceiling of the ship in the room where the two hundred immigrant passengers were huddled, gave way with the pounding of the waves. Metal dishes and personal effects flew about the room as the passengers screamed in terror. There were no lights and the passengers scrambled in their attempt to remain upright. It was pitch black and the middle of the night. A woman and child of the group perished. The crew members came down to this hell on the sea and gave up the bodies of the deceased to the angry sea. An old man who was travelling with them, Habib Abood, was violently ill, and asked Tom and another passenger, Sam Courie, to assist him to the deck for some fresh air. The two young men agreed and helped the old man to the deck of the ship. As they stepped onto the deck the ship pitched to a forty-five degree angle and the three men fell to the deck and were instantly being rolled to its edge. The captain and his crew were holding on to the life lines that had been rigged on the open deck to allow the crew to move to the mid deck where the wheel house was located. They saw the three passengers and caught them before they rolled into the sea. They were dragged back to the steps leading to the hold and with angry words from the captain were told to get below. The captain warned them that if they did not stay below they would be put into the brig. The storm raged for seven days and when the seas were again calm the battered passengers from the bowels of the ship came up for some clean sea air.

Twenty days after leaving Cherborg the ship docked in St. Thomas, Tom and his companions walked off the ship and onto the land with joy in their hearts that they had made this part of their trip safely. St. Thomas in the year of 1910 was controlled by the Danish government. Most of the immigrants were without money at this point, and Tom was one of the ones who had no money. He contacted his uncle John, who was in Cedar Rapids, Iowa and asked that some money be wired to him. His uncle promptly wired Tom one hundred and fifty dollars. The thirty members of the group who were travelling together from Lebanon discussed their plight with the head of the group, George David, and he told them that they would have to be smuggled through the countries of Central America to get to Mexico where they would be able to enter the United States through the state of Texas. He explained to them that they had no papers to travel through the Central American countries and therefore they could not be seen in daylight for if they were they would be arrested.

The group had become bedraggled and tired and after twenty days on the ship being feed subpar food they were constantly hungry. They had little money and decided that they would have to stick together with their leader if they were to get to America at all, so they agreed with Mr. David that they would do whatever was necessary to complete their trip. The ship continued its route to Costa Rica and stopped at several islands along the way. Tom and his companions were able to fish at the stops that were made and ate the fish that they caught, after the horrible food that they had existed on during their trip from Cherborg to St. Thomas, it was a welcome change in their diet. When they arrived in Costa Rica, Mr. David made arrangements for them to sleep in a cheap hotel and most of the group slept on the bare wood floors so that many of them could share the less than adequate shelter.

After being hidden for several days in Costa Rica the weary travellers were told that they would have to walk on the next leg of their journey, so after dark they set out with their meager belongings and with no understanding of what was being asked of them. They did not know that their destination was miles away and that it would be weeks before they would have any facilities to bathe, eat a hot meal or rest in comfort. They walked by night and slept hidden in the woods by day. They were warned that they must not speak to anyone that they might meet as they were not legally in the countries through which they were passing. The Central American countries through which they were passing were very close to the equator and the heat both days and nights was oppressive. Several of the immigrants became ill and the others would wait for them to recover before they could continue their journey. As each hot day passed into the next the immigrants lost track of time and clung to the belief that they would soon reach their destination. The wooded areas of the countries of Central America were jungles, filled with wild animals and the immigrants were forced to travel through these unsafe woods so that they would not be detected. The chattering of the parrots, the howls of the wild animals, and the steady bedlam robbed them of sleep and when they travelled at night they lived in constant fear for their lives in a land where they did not speak the language, did not know the customs and were illegal intruders.

After several days they found a railroad track and when the trainmen were not looking they crawled into empty boxcars so that they could cover a few more miles of their journey. Before the trains pulled into their destination the immigrants would jump off and hide until another opportunity appeared for them to have more means of transportation. They often begged rides from the caravans of ox-carts that were carrying coffee beans to the railroads for shipment to the United States. As they went further and further into the countryside they often were able to beg rides from passing farmers with their wagons who did not know that the group were illegally in their country. At one point Tom and a companion decided to walk ahead to a railroad station that they had been told about. They walked onto a railroad trestle that ran over a river, thinking that the walking would be easier. They were trapped on the trestle as a train approached. The two men ran furiously to the other end of the trestle and just as the train bore down on them they were able to jump from the track into a gully where they laid breathlessly after their near disaster.

Wherever they could they bought small supplies of food and ate along the road supplementing their food hoard with whatever they found along the way that was edible. After three weeks of walking, riding trains, donkeys, horses and in wagons, they made their way through Costa Rica, Honduras, and Nicaragua to Mexico City. There they were taken in by members of the people who were herding immigrants to the United States. George David, who was receiving a commission for each immigrant that he led to the United States continued with Tom and several of the other immigrants to El Paso. Fedwa and Tom Shaheen, who were travelling with the group were directed to Laredo, Texas, as their father would meet them there.

When Tom and his group reached El Paso, Texas, on December 27, 1910, they were met by the network of people who worked with immigration groups and after being checked for any illnesses were directed to a passage house, where immigrants were housed and herded on their way to the destination of people who were sponsoring them. Tom was taken to the home of a Mrs. Malooli who showed him the bathroom and told him to take a bath. After nearly four months on the road Tom badly needed a bath. He had never taken a bath in a tub before and was intrigued with the first custom that he experienced in this new country of his. Mrs. Malooli, gave him his supper and Tom had his first night's sleep in a bed since he left home. The next morning he was directed to the railroad station to board a train to Cedar Rapids, Iowa where his uncles Mike and John, were waiting for him.

The train stopped in St. Joseph, Missouri and Tom was taken to another of the houses that handled immigrants. Here he was again instructed to take a bath. Tom thought that these strange people were very determined to keep him clean. After some more meals and a good night's sleep, Tom reboarded the train and travelled the last leg of his long journey to meet his uncles. On January 1,1911 Tom arrived in the Cedar Rapids, Iowa railroad station. As he walked out of the station he saw a man in a uniform and knew that he was a policeman. He showed the officer a piece of paper that he was carrying that had his uncles' address on it. The officer who could not communicate with Tom because of the language barrier pointed in a direction and motioned for Tom to go that way. Tom found a man driving a horse and buggy and tried to ask the man to take him to his uncles' home but the man pointed in the other direction and Tom was left standing on the street corner, in the middle of the winter, with the temperature below zero, wearing the light clothes that he had been wearing in the hot climates that he travelled. He stopped a boy on a bicycle and once again sought to get directions to his destination. The boy motioned Tom to follow him and Tom arrived at the door of his uncles' grocery store. He stood in the doorway and his relatives stared at him in disbelief. After several months of not hearing from him they had decided that he had been lost for good. As the reality of Tom standing before them sunk in they began to shout and cry with relief that he had made it. Tom too started to cry with relief that members of his extended family were actually in his grasp.

Uncle Mike and Uncle John brought Tom into their living quarters which were behind the store and fed him a hot meal. Tom ate hungrily, as this was the first Lebanese food that he had had since leaving Ain Arab four months earlier. After several days of resting and telling his relatives of his trip Tom asked his uncles if there was work for him in his new country. His uncle John told Tom that for several months he would let him work in the store so that Tom could learn to speak some of the English language and to get used to the Americans that would be his customers and neighbors.

X

     Tom was eager to learn and listened carefully when his relatives talked to their customers who came into the store on a daily basis. After two months of learning how to sell and how to speak to the customers Uncle Mike told Tom that he would like him to go out on the road with Uncle John to learn to be a peddler. Uncle John and Uncle Mike travelled throughout the country farms in northern Iowa and southern Minnesota selling merchandise from their general store in Cedar Rapids, Iowa. They provided this service as the farmers in the area could not make many trips to town when they were in the midst of their growing season or were busy with the dairy cows year-round. Tom looked at his uncle apprehensively as he was not sure that he could sell to the mainly Scandinavian descendants who were the farmers in these midwestern lands of the United States. That night as he lay in his bed Tom thought of the things that he would do to try to be successful in his new job. He would always be honest and trustworthy, he would be polite to his customers and he would be sincere when trying to convince his customers that they needed his wares. The next morning after eating his breakfast, Tom helped his uncle Mike to pack a backpack of merchandise that he would carry and try to sell to the farmwives on his route. His Uncle John took him out to the countryside and brought Tom to some of the farms so that he could show him how to speak to the farmers and how to sell his merchandise. At the end of the first day Uncle John stopped at a farmhouse and asked for lodging for the night. The farmer told them that they could stay for the night and invited them to have supper with them. After supper Tom went out into the yard to join the farmers sons as it was still daylight. The young farm boys realized that Tom could not speak very much English and decided that it would be fun to teach him some profanity. Tom, did not know what he was being taught to say and was very proud of the fact that he could learn these words so easily. Later, Uncle Mike came out to the yard to check on Tom's whereabouts and heard Tom swearing. He became very angry and began to chastise Tom. Tom was bewildered as he did not know what he had done wrong. The farm boys, seeing that Tom was in trouble with his uncle came over to them and explained to Uncle Mike that they had taught Tom the swear words and apologized. Uncle Mike then understood and explained to Tom why he had become angry with him. The next day, they continued on their route and Uncle John continued to teach Tom to sell. After two days Uncle John took Tom to a crossroads and told him to take a road that led away from the crossroad where they were stopped. He told Tom that he was to visit the farms on that road and was to meet him at the next crossroad that he came to. Tom started off in the wet and melting snow that lay on the ground. As his uncle disappeared from view Tom thought of his father's words, that he would have to face the world alone and have no one to depend on. At that moment as a wave of loneliness swept over him he felt very much alone, but he gritted his teeth and vowed that he would make his uncles, who had become his surrogate fathers, proud of him. His shoes soon became saturated with water as he did not have any boots on his feet. As the day wore on his feet became colder and colder.

The first farm wife that he encountered as he walked up the road to her farm told him that she did not need any goods that day and Tom went on to the next farm. He saw the farmer riding his tractor by the roadside and Tom went up to him and asked him if he would like to buy some merchandise. The farmer looked at the cold and earnest young man and asked to see his wares. Tom showed him the things that he was carrying in his backpack and the farmer decided to buy six silver spoons from Tom. Tom charged him one dollar and twenty-five cents. As he went down the road after his very first sale, he began to wonder if he had sold the spoons at a profit so he stopped by the roadside and checked the invoices that he had for the merchandise. He realized that he had made a fifty cent profit and was elated. Tom continued down the road stopping at each of the farmhouses and trying to sells his goods. He had no more luck and after several hours of trudging through the snow he reached the crossroad where his uncle had told him to meet him. Uncle John was waiting for him and as he walked up to him Uncle John said "how was business?" and Tom replied, "good! good!". But, Tom noticed a train passing by the roadside. He said to his uncle, "where is that train going?", and his uncle John answered, "it is going to Cedar Rapids." and Tom said, "Please let me get on the train and go back to Cedar Rapids, I do not think that I want to be a peddler and there must be a better way for me to make a living. My feet are wet because I do not have overshoes and if you let me go back to Uncle Mike's store I will work there and if I do not do well, I will go back to Ain Arab and will help my father to tend the goats." Uncle John looked at his young nephew and said, "I suppose you would like a job in a bank" but he decided to let Tom board the train and return to Cedar Rapids. When Tom arrived back at Uncle Mike's store later that evening his uncle was startled to see him. He asked Tom why he had returned and Tom told him that he would like to work in the store instead of on the road. His uncle looked at him and decided that he would give Tom a little more time to get used to selling to people. He also told Tom that he would buy him a horse and wagon so that he did not have to walk. After several more weeks of working in the store Uncle Mike told Tom that he would once again have to go out on the road and learn to sell. Tom felt a little more confident and with the horse and wagon and Uncle John's instruction he once again set out on a route of farms to sell his wares. He was a likable young fellow and soon realized that his father's words of advice on how to get along with people worked very well. He was polite and respectful and soon found out that he could sell the merchandise that his uncles had given him to sell. When he returned to Cedar Rapids he had made seventy-five dollars profit and his uncles told him that he was doing well and would be a good peddler.

Tom, began to feel a little more confident of his future and soon found that he could learn the ways of this new and strange country to which he had come. He soon fell into a routine of selling on the road to the farmers of the region. He learned that, although they were of a different background than his that if he followed his father's advice he could succeed. His daily experiences were teaching him how to make his living and how to get along with people.

The sun rose bright and shining and Tom set out for his rounds. He visited several farms and sold several pieces of merchandise. As the afternoon wore on he looked for a farm that would give him lodging for the night. A Swedish farmer who had purchased a pair of work gloves from Tom admired the young man's manners and spunk and told him that he could spend the night there. The next morning Tom went to the barn to watch the farmer and his sons milk the cows. He offered to help, thinking that this would show the farmer that he appreciated his letting him stay the night. The two farm boys looked at each other and smiled. They gave Tom a milking stool and told him to milk one of the cows. They did not tell him that the cow was very high strung and had to be approached gently. Tom, sat on the stool and began to vigorously milk the cow. She was unhappy with the strange hands on her udders and immediately kicked back. Tom was kicked from the stool as the pail of milk flew into the air. He landed in a pile of cow manure and the spilled milk landed on top of him. As he lay in the manure drenched with the milk the farmer entered the barn and saw his sons laughing at Tom. He immediately scolded his sons and told them to give Tom some of their clean clothes to change into and told Tom to go into the barn and clean himself up. Tom did so and realized that the farm boys were just having some fun at his expense.

He continued to improve and after several months of travelling to the farms and selling he began to win over many of his Uncle John's customers. The farmers admired this honest and hard working young man and he was treated well by them. His Uncle John was amused that Tom was winning his customers over and, encouraged him to make as much as he could. After a year Tom decided that he would buy a pair of Arabian horses to go with his wagon and as he travelled his route the farmers came to see his fine horses and admire them. Tom, who had paid seven hundred and fifty dollars for the animals used the farmers interest in them to sell them his wares. His profits increased and after two years of working he decided that at the age of twenty, he should be thinking of getting married. He looked around to see if there were any single young women who lived in the area that would make a suitable wife for him and met a young woman named Ann whose father was one of Uncle Mike's customers. He began to visit her and properly chaperoned escorted her to dinner. After several dates her father confronted Tom and asked what his intentions were toward his daughter. Tom told him that he was looking for a wife and Ann's father asked Tom what his financial status was and if he realized what it cost to support a wife. Tom said, "to tell you the truth I do not have very much and as a matter of fact this derby hat on my head belongs to my uncle", which was true. Tom was insulted at the man's questions and left. He never went back to see the girl. But, he continued to think about getting married and one night as he slept, he saw the girl in his dreams that had make the trip from Ain Arab with his group. She was tall, slender and had a beautiful figure. Tom smiled to himself in his dream and decided that he had at last found someone suitable to marry.

XI

It was the fall of 1912 and Tom had been in the United States for almost two years. He had learned enough of the customs and language of his new country to be comfortable in dealing with his customers on his peddler's route. He had applied his father's philosophy of honesty, politeness and friendliness and had associated with people of good moral character, and he had become a very successful peddler. He had learned that the mostly Scandinavian farmers that he sold to were hard working, honest and successful so that they recognized that he lived up to the same standards that they held for themselves. And although they were of a different ethnic background than he, they bought his wares and trusted him as one of their own.

Tom told his uncle Mike of the girl in his dream who, with her brother Tom Shaheen, had traveled to the United States with his group from Lebanon. He told his uncle that in his dream he realized that this was the girl that he should marry. His uncle smiled and told Tom that he could take some time off from selling wares to the farmers of the region and go to Blue Earth, Minnesota where this girl Fedwa, now called Frances, lived and talk to her father. Joseph and Sadie Shaheen were the parents of this girl Frances that interested Tom. He took some of his money that he had saved from his earnings and bought a ticket for the train ride to Blue Earth to convince Frances' father that he would be a good husband to his daughter and a good son-in-law.

When Tom arrived in Blue Earth he took a small room at a boarding house and inquired of the townspeople where the Shaheens lived. He went to the house and introduced himself and, as he was a Lebanese just like the Shaheens, was warmly welcomed. Several days later Tom went to the school, where Frances was a student at the time, when she would be leaving for home. As she walked down the steps of the school Tom gazed at her. She was tall, slender and carried herself with dignity and serenity. Tom was very sure that this was the girl that he wanted for his wife. Tom visited the Shaheen family several times and finally mustered enough courage to tell Frances' father why he had come to their town, that he wished to marry Joseph's daughter. Joseph Shaheen realized that this earnest young man would be a good husband for his daughter but was concerned with the fact that she was only fifteen years old, having been born on April 14, 1898 in Ain Arab, Lebanon. However, he allowed Tom to visit his daughter under supervision and soon realized that his daughter was growing to love this Tom Haddy. The relationship grew and Frances' father Joseph gave Tom permission to marry his daughter.

Frances' mother Sadie began to prepare for the marriage of her daughter. The traditions of the Lebanese culture must be a part of this wedding she thought. Because Frances was so young, Sadie had to hurry to prepare her daughter's dowry. No true Lebanese young woman went to her marriage without her dowry which included personal household items, and her personal linens for her future home. The Shaheens and their friends and members of Tom's extended family in Cedar Rapids, Iowa gathered for the wedding.

The festivities lasted for several days before the wedding as was tradition in Lebanese families. The women friends of the Shaheens sang wedding songs known in the arabic language as zalagheet. Verses in these songs welcomed the wedding guests and proposed a toast to the parents of the bride, "Ah wee, ahla sahla bil thyoof, as wee niskee il ahal wal thyoor'.

On February 22, 1913, the birthday of George Washington, the father of Tom's adopted country, Frances and Tom were married in Blue Earth, Minnesota. Tom's only regret at this time was that his family in Ain Arab were far away and could not be with him on this joyous occasion of his marriage. The Shaheens' family and friends celebrated with parties known in Arabic as sahras. There was feasting, and dancing of an Arabic dance called the dubkee. There was eating of Lebanese pastry delicacies and nuts were served to the guests. The candy-coated almond served at weddings signifies a sweet and prosperous life.

The Shaheens served their guests a traditional Lebanese dinner after the ceremony which included kibby, roz and batinjam mihshee. As they left, the guests bade Tom and his bride good-bye by saying 'nikshalak arees' which is Arabic for the saying 'may you be blessed with a boy'.

As Blue Earth did not have an Orthodox Church where Lebanese and Syrian families traditionally worshipped, Tom and Frances were married in the Roman Catholic church of the town. Frances' mother, Sadie Shaheen was not happy that her only daughters' marriage had not been blessed by an orthodox priest and insisted that Tom and Frances not 'consummate' their marriage until it was blessed properly. Tom, who was eager to have his new in-laws approve of him and his character, suggested that he and his new bride return to Cedar Rapids, Iowa where an orthodox priest would remarry him and his young bride. So, properly chaperoned the young husband and his bride traveled the train ride to Cedar Rapids for his honeymoon. After being remarried and receiving the blessings of the Orthodox church to satisfy Sadie, the young newlyweds returned to Blue Earth to live with Tom's in-laws, where Tom, now an experienced peddler bought a team of handsome horses and a wagon and continued his career of selling wares to the farmers of the area of his new home.

There were several members of his extended Lebanese family in the area who were general store owners as were his Uncles Mike and John in Cedar Rapids and Tom bought his stock from them and they soon realized that this earnest young man could be trusted and was a diligent and honest tradesman.

One and one-half years later, Tom, like his father before him was eagerly awaiting the birth of his first child. His first American. On September 16, 1915 Tom and Frances were blessed with their first child, whom they named Elizabeth Julia. And Tom, like his father before him, knelt and thanked his God for this gift of a child. He then wrote to tell his father and mother that the first of a new generation of their family had 'seen the sun' for the first time and he was sure that this first American would carry on the honor and traditions of the Haddy family. His parents responded that they were delighted on hearing the news of his first-born and were saddened that they could not be with him at this most important time of his life.

Tom continued to work as a peddler and in 1916 Joe Shaheen, Tom's father-in-law, suggested that he and Tom open a store in the village of Walters, Minnesota, a town that was about ten miles from the border between Minnesota and Iowa. The area consisted of black and fertile farmland with thick nutrient filled soil. The farmers of the area, who were mostly of Scandinavian and German descent, worked the land prosperously and they had settled in southern Minnesota because its soil was much like the rich soil of their ancestors' native countries of Germany, Norway, Sweden and Finland. Tom Haddy and Joe Shaheens' store would be the third general store in this town and they would have to work hard to meet the existing competition. But Tom was excited at the prospect of owning his own store and vowed that he would work to meet the competition, so he and his father-in-law, with a startup capital of fifteen hundred dollars opened their new store.

The two men bought two trucks and each of them would run the trucks out to the farms, five days a week, to buy the farmers eggs and sell them their groceries. One of the other stores, that was located in Walters ahead of them would go bankrupt but the Shaheen-Haddy store would survive and prosper, for Tom believed that faith and a belief in oneself was one of the keys to success.

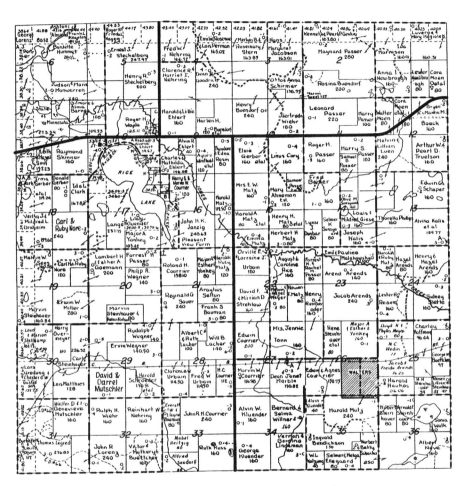

FOSTER 1864
TOWNSHIP 1964

XII

In 1900 the ton, Cedar Rapids and Northern railroad built a line of track from Germania, Iowa to Albert Lea, Minnesota. Walters was a new little town founded on this railroad line and was located in Fairbault County. The railroad would later change its name to the Chicago Rock Island and Pacific. The railroad line skirted a little town called Bricelyn, then went across Seely township, through the township of Brush Creek and on through Foster township on its route to Albert Lea. The site of Walters was identified as section 26 in Foster township. Thomas H. Brown, who owned this piece of land, filed a plat on August 15, 1900 at the Fairbault county register of deeds, to establish a village on his land. Three years later in 1903 Walters was incorporated as a village.

The officials of the railroad company picked the name of Walters for the new town but later would ask that the name be changed because the railroad had a town of Walters, Oklahoma on its route and the mail bags for the two towns were often mixed up. When railroad officials asked that the name of the town be changed to avoid the confusion with the other town of Walters, area residents submitted substitute names but the original name of Walters was retained. Many residents of the town thought that this would be a good opportunity to give note to family names or names of favorite sons. Submitted as substitute names were Meiggs Station, Ludtkefast, Kliebensteinburgh, Yostown, Meyerapolis, and Ruppfort.

At the end of November in 1900 the town boasted a general store, a saloon, a grain elevator, a bank, a lumberyard, a restaurant, and a combined livery and feed barn. At the end of 1906 there was a schoolhouse, a hardware store, a second elevator, more saloons, a post office, two general stores, a hotel, a creamery, a pool hall, a drayline, a second lumberyard, a blacksmith, a drug store, and a harness shop. On January 19, 1901 a post-office opened with one Fred Hartman as the first postmaster. Walters built a two-story building for its first schoolhouse in

1906 and was part of school district number 83. A one room rural school a half a mile southwest of the township was moved into the town and was temporarily used until the new school was ready on September 17, 1906.

During the first half of the decade of the existence of Walters a famous local story was of a tornado that lifted the school and the children inside it over a fence and deposited it in a pasture. No one, fortunately, was hurt. In 1904 a town cemetery was added and Thomas H. Brown started a weekly newspaper in the town and called it The News. One Alma Scott was the first editor of the paper but unfortunately publication of the paper was soon suspended. Some street lamps were installed in 1908 and electric lights were installed in 1919. The first sidewalks were made of planks but the heavy threshing machines which passed over them caused problems so an ordinance was passed forbidding the threshers to pass over the sidewalks. In 1909 crushed rock was hauled in and spread about the streets. The workmen who did the work were paid three dollars for one and one half days work. In 1905 Walters would start a school band that would become well known. The band played at all of the local affairs, Fourth of July celebrations, fairs and other special events. The population of Walters grew to 102 people in 1910 and to 116 in 1920 and to 152 in 1970. In the year 1976 this little historic town of the mid-west would be designated as a Bicentennial site.

Main Street - Plank sidewalk - 1915

Walters Street Scene - 1909

XIII

Tom and Frances and their daughter Elizabeth lived in a house with Frances' mother and father, her sister Selma and brothers George and Tom and he was delighted at the way that his life in this new land called America was progressing. The house that they lived in was owned by a family named Steinhauer and was located on the west side of Walters. In less than six years in this new land he had learned to sell merchandise to the farmers of the midwestern part of this country and now he would advance to learning how to operate a general store in this town of Walters, Minnesota. Before he went to bed at night, he would kneel at his bedside and thank his God for his good fortune and ask that he be given the strength and wisdom to be a good store-owner and to serve his customers well. He also would vow to live by his father's words and continue to be an honorable man.

As the first year of business ended Tom began to think of how he could ensure that his career as a general store manager in this small midwestern town, would be successful. He watched as the other merchants in the town conducted their business and soon realized that if he was to be successful in this new job he would have to get involved in the town life of his customers. Slowly, he began to offer his services when community projects were discussed and planned by the people who ran the town. He was polite and sincere in his efforts and gradually began to know more and more of the townspeople. They in turn would buy his wares and soon he was a known and respected tradesman.

Spring was in the air on this April 4th in the year of 1917 and the snows were beginning to melt. Tom was happy because Frances was soon to have their second child. As he walked through this small town of Walters that he called home Tom reflected upon becoming a father for the second time. The sky was ablaze with stars, there was a chill in the air, and Tom felt contentment as he walked toward his home. As he walked he thought to himself that he was indeed a rich man for as he approached the door of his home he knew that on the other side was someone who loved him and believed in him. Someone who stood by his side and devoted herself to him and to creating their family. A man was truly blessed to have such a life's partner. He thought of his father, far away in Ain Arab and wished that he could talk to him now and ask him if he was living up to the standards that his father had taught him of being an honorable and strong man. He smiled to himself and knew that his father would be pleased with his progress in his life's work. As he approached the house he saw that the doctor's Ford was parked nearby and knew that Frances was giving birth to their child and ran into the house and rushed up the steps to their bedroom. The doctor was preparing Frances as she was just beginning to give birth to their second child. Tom paced nervously in the kitchen as the doctor attended Frances in her delivery.

He soon heard the cries of his new child and smiled as the doctor came into the kitchen to tell him that he had a new baby girl. Tom went into the bedroom where Frances lay and saw her cradling the child in her arms. He bent to kiss his wife and she smiled and said, "Isn't she beautiful". Tom smiled and nodded his agreement. Frances then said, "Let's call her Beatrice Virginia". Tom laughed and agreed that his second child would be called Beatrice. He picked the child up and cradled her in his large hands and silently thanked his God for this gift of a child.

XIV

When Tom and his father-in-law opened their grocery store in Walters there were two competitors ahead of them, a Mr. Jim Logan and a Mr. O.H. Koetke. Now, Mr. Jim Logan was moving out of his store. Tom and O.H. Koetke had been sharing an entrance to the building that they shared and as competitors it had sometimes been awkward in dealing with the farmers who brought eggs to be sold to the two businesses. Tom, Frances and her father talked about Mr. Logan moving out of his store which was located in another building in town and was a corner location, and decided that that store was bigger and would enable them to expand the business. They purchased the second location for their store in Walters from Mr. Logan and moved from the old building to the corner location. Tom thought, 'this is another step up to enlarge the business and prosper'.

One year later in 1921 Tom's father-in-law, Joe Shaheen opened a second store in Conger, nine miles from Walters. The two stores worked together and pooled resources for success. And in this memorable year Tom would become a naturalized citizen of his adopted homeland. Frances would also become a citizen and they were deeply proud of their new status.

At this time in his life Tom and Frances had moved into a house owned by the Meyer family of the town of Walters. They also now had four children, as Lucille Mae, who was born on May 10, 1918, had joined them and Joseph George, who was born on March 17, 1920, had increased their children's number to four. Tom thought, 'When I came to Walters the population of the town was 96, we Haddys have increased that number by four new residents to our hometown'.

On September 6, 1922 Frances would bear another son for Tom. This time he would not be there for the birth as he had taken the train to Minneapolis to buy supplies for the store, but he and Frances had agreed that if their next child was a boy he could name it after himself and call it Tom. Frances was very irate that Tom had planned his trip without thinking that their next might child might arrive at any moment. The doctor came to assist her and other female friends came to help her also as they knew that Tom was away. To get back at him for his absence Frances thought that she would name this child after herself and did so by calling him Francis John. When Tom got home he was delighted at the birth of his second son but disappointed that the boy would not be named after himself. He would have to wait for the next "boy" he thought.

Over the next several years Tom worked to make his store a success. He became more involved in the community and with his good friend O.H. Koetke worked to improve the town's well-being. He and O.H. talked about ways to expand business without hurting the other fellow. They talked about a plan to organize the egg dealers in their town and the surrounding towns into an egg-dealers association so that they could all profit if they got together. They contacted the other egg dealers in surrounding towns and proposed that they gather together for the good of all and to work to improve the egg business in the area. The other businessmen were delighted to join. By cooperating to solve their problems they were able to stabilize the egg business in the area and prosper. It was to be the first egg business association in their area of southern Minnesota. Tom thought back to the early years in Ain Arab when his father would join together with the other goatherders to care for the flocks and ward off the attacks of the Druse. This egg association would use the same philosophy of working together for the good of all.

During this period in his career Tom was very happy that the Jack Sprat company, which was a large national company had contacted him to ask him to represent the company's products in the town of Walters. Tom stocked Jack Sprat food products and became their representative in the town. This increased his business and stature in the town. His store was one of six in the southern Minnesota area to be a representative of Jack Sprat. The Jack Sprat company was promoting advertising for 125 stores in the state of Minnesota and Tom benefited from this association.

Tom decided to join the independent softball team of the town of Walters. They belonged to a league of the neighboring towns. The old injury that he had suffered at the hands of the Druse in the early years of his life had left his right elbow locked so that he could not bend his arm. But he could throw a softball underhanded with a great deal of speed, faster than others could throw it overhanded, and he soon became an expert pitcher for the team. The team won many championships with Tom as their pitcher and his friend O.H. Koetke played on the team with him.

One day Tom and O.H. were talking about all of the farmers who came to town on Saturday night to deliver their eggs to the merchants and to shop for the groceries and supplies that they and their families needed. They thought that if they could provide entertainment to these farmers and their families when they came to town it would create good will and help business. The side of the store building was a bare wall and the two men thought that it would make a good movie screen. So they contacted a dealer in Minneapolis who rented movie reels and set up an outdoor theater for the farmers and their families to watch movies on their visits to Walters on Saturday nights. The idea was a big success and became a social gathering time for the farmers in the area. Picnic lunches were brought to town and as the farmers waited for the business people to handle the eggs that they brought to town to sell and to fill their orders for groceries and supplies, they had an enjoyable time watching movies and having a picnic sitting in the grass outside the store. Western movies were the most popular with those who watched these shows. The friendship and respect between the farmers and the town business people grew and the sense of community was strengthened.

Although Tom and O.H. were competitors in business they were friends and worked together for the good of the town which was good for each business. They were pioneers in the concept that businesses are a part of the community which they serve and that they should become involved in the life of the townspeople and act on behalf of their customers to improve their lives and the prosperity of the town.

Tom and Frances lives were enriched by their becoming a part of the community and being respected by the townspeople and the farmers of the surrounding area. Their children attended the local school and were happy, healthy and contented. The town did not have an orthodox church that most Lebanese attended but Tom and Frances thought that it was important that their children grow up with attending church as a part of their upbringing so they insisted that all of the family attend the Lutheran church in the town on Sunday mornings. The family became involved in the church activities but the children were taken to Cedar Rapids, Iowa, where they were confirmed in that city's orthodox church.

Frances' happiest times were when her children were in school and she would attend all of their special activities. She helped Tom in his business by working in the dry goods section of the store, and as she was a good seamstress she took care of the yard goods that they sold. She also sold the hosiery and acted as the bookkeeper for the store. Tom served as treasurer for the school that his children attended for many years. He was physically strong and worked long hours in the store often lifting heavy loads by himself. In addition to buying the eggs from the farmers in the area he bought their poultry. Often, Tom bartered with his customers, giving them groceries and drygoods for their eggs and poultry.

The produce that he sold came from Albert Lea, a town reasonably close by, which had a wholesale warehouse for groceries. He made trips to Minneapolis and St. Paul, two fairly large cities, to purchase clothes and other merchandise, such as, ladies ready to wear, overalls, dry goods and yardage, from the G. Sommers and Butler Brothers companies. And he kept a truck and a car to use for the business. His car was a Reo open touring car. One day on a trip to Conger he got stuck on a road while caught in a rain storm. The country roads that he was travelling were black gumbo mud and people could hear the roaring of the engine as Tom tried to get started. He thought back to his peddler days and went to a farmer's house for the night. He had gone from a pack on his back, to a horse and a wagon, a horse and a buggy and a horse and a large wagon, to a car and truck and he still occasionally got stuck in the mud, just as he had in the early days of his career. And his life was still tied to the Scandinavian and German farmers of the area who, although he was a dark-skinned Lebanese and not of their culture, had grown to respect him and accept him as one of their own.

It was September 24, 1924 and Tom was once again eagerly awaiting the birth of a child. He was excited as the doctor had told him and Frances that she might be waiting for twins. He once again said a prayer that these children would be healthy. He thought back to two years before on September 6, 1922 when his second son Francis has been born. The son who was to have been named after him but whom Frances had named after herself in to get back at him for not having been present. Tom chuckled as he thought of his wife's spunky nature.

Frances did indeed present Tom with twin daughters, who were named Juanita Rose and Vernita Rosella, and now he was the proud father of seven healthy children. A good substantial Lebanese family he thought. He began to think that maybe there would be no more children and no more sons to carry his name but he smiled at Frances' ploy of naming their second son after her for his missing that son's birth and thought that he was blessed to have the seven beautiful and healthy children that he had.

Almost a year after the birth of the twins Tom renovated the top floor of the store and moved his family into the apartment that was created. This was a more economical way to provide for his large family. As Tom's circle of friends expanded in the town he came to know his customers not only as customers but as a part of his life. One customer named Peter Haukoos had fourteen children and often came to Tom's store to visit as well as to buy. One day Pete came into the store and told Tom that he needed work shirts for his boys. When Tom asked him what size he needed he said, 'give me what you have and I will fit them to the boys'.

On another of Pete's visits he asked Tom why he did not carry oleomargarine, a lard-like product that was colored yellow with a packet of yellow food coloring and was sold as a substitute for butter. Pete was a member of the board of directors of the creamery association of the area. So Tom agreed to carry oleomargarine in his store if Pete would buy all of the stock of oleomargarine that Tom had on hand if the other board members objected to Tom's selling the product. Henry Sauer, another townsman who was on the creamery board threatened not to deal with Tom if he sold oleomargarine so Pete kept his promise and bought the two cases that Tom had on hand as a result of his request that Tom sell oleomargarine.

XV

As the years went by Tom realized that he was raising a family of Americans. His children, who were growing up in the heartland of America were adopting the customs and culture of their surroundings. And although they were taught the roots of their origins at home and were absorbing the tenets of these roots their outlook on life was also being influenced by the Americanization that was taking place in them in their school and in the town. But it did not really bother Tom that his children were being Americanized as he believed that his philosophy, like that of his father before him, to be of good character and work hard, was valid no matter what culture one grew up in. He also knew that every immigrant to this country was raising Americans, and although each ethnic group treasured the culture of their homeland, their children would grow absorbing the culture of their ancestors and the culture of their native-born country, America. This blending of cultures in new born Americans of immigrant parents would give America her diversity, strength and character.

He was fascinated by the differences in the seven children he and Frances had created, the girls, Elizabeth, Beatrice, Lucille, Juanita and Vernita, were vibrant and eager but were also caring and gentle like their mother. Francis was a curious child who liked to learn all that he could and Tom recognized the same stubborn determination in his son Joe as was in him when he grew up in Ain Arab, the stubbornness and determination that had led to his decision to leave Ain Arab to come to America. Joe was high spirited and one day, as he often did Joe went off with a friend to the boy's family farm and did not return for many hours in spite of the fact that Tom had told him not to go. When Joe returned Tom decided that the boy should be punished but when he went to give him the spanking that Tom thought that the boy deserved, Joe ran away from his father's wrath. Tom chased Joe through the alley next to the store and finally caught him. He then thrashed the boy to teach him that he should obey his father's wishes. Tom believed that if he was strict, but fair, with his children they would learn important lessons about how to behave as a member of society. These lessons would be important for their future success as adults.

It was the year 1929 and as Tom walked through the town he was deep in thought. The election of the town mayor was coming up and Tom thought that maybe he should run for the post. As he returned home he decided that he would run for mayor and would talk to Frances to see if she agreed that he should try for the mayor's position. Frances was supportive of his idea and told him that he should talk to some of the townspeople to see if they would support him. Tom contacted his friend O.H. to see what he thought of the idea and his friend told him that he would support him if he should decide to run. Tom gathered his friend's together and organized a modest campaign of posters and flyers to advertise his candidacy. He talked to many townspeople and asked for their support. Most knew and trusted Tom after many years of working with him and his service to them by providing goods and services to the families in the town and the farmers in the outlying areas of Walters.

When the election was over Tom was surprised and excited. He had won the election as town Mayor and would have an opportunity to make decisions to help the town to improve. Any improvements that could be made for the town would be good for business, for as the town improved and its people prospered, Tom knew that the business would prosper too.

He had been involved with many projects in the town and now would have the opportunity to suggest more improvements and create more good will by expanding his service to the area. Nearby towns were installing poles and equipment for electricity to be brought to their town. Several of the town's leaders in business and finance thought that Walters would benefit from having electricity. The town had had electricity on a limited basis since 1919, provided by a man who owned a small generator. So as mayor, on November 5, 1929 Tom and his fellow businessmen held a vote. The townspeople voted forty-four to seven in favor of bringing electricity to Walters. The backers of the town thought that about three thousand dollars would be needed to bring electricity to Walters. They thought of selling town bonds to cover the cost of paying for the Interstate Power Company of Albert Lea, Minnesota to bring in the lights. But the attorneys hired by the townsmen, Front and Morris of Blue Earth, Minnesota told the men that they could get the electricity without having to pay for it to be brought to Walters. A hearing was held in the town and the power company agreed to install the lights at no charge. People in the town were excited at having electricity in their town.

Selling of beer was legal in the town of Walters when Tom was Mayor but he would not condone driving recklessly through the town when someone was drunk and often had drunk drivers put into the town jail. His son Joe used to spend time watching the drunks in the jail beat on the bars with their tin cups.

Later, O.H. and Tom decided that spotlights should be installed at Walters Park so that night games of softball could be played. Another opportunity for the townspeople and people of the surrounding area to have a source of social activity was achieved and another link in the bonds of friendship for these people was forged.

At the end of the year 1930, Tom and Frances did an inventory of their business and were delighted that they had earned $2500 that year. Their lives had taken on a pleasant smoothness with healthy children and a business that was a part of their adopted town. Their children were active in school and the events sponsored by the town, they had successfully integrated their lives into that of the townspeople. They were well on their way to achieving the 'American Dream' of prosperity that most of the immigrants in those early years of the building of America worked toward.

O.H. and Tom met and were discussing what many townspeople were talking about. The town needed a bank. They discussed how a bank could be opened in Walters and decided that money had to be raised to support this latest venture. And on January 1, 1931 it was announced that a bank was to be opened in the town of Walters. Its name would be the Farmers and Merchants State Bank of Walters. They joined together and with other businessmen sold stock to raise the money to back the establishment of the bank. The town received a charter on December 22, 1931 and the money that the businessmen of the town had raised selling stock provided capital of $20,000. The initial officers and Board of Directors were Henry Motz, President; Bill Katzung, Vice President; Mr. Larson, Cashier; and O.H. Koetke and TJ. Haddy as board members.

This farm stood where Keister stands today. Originally homesteaded by
Joseph E Wind in 1872, it was sold to Conrad Wipplinger in January
1894. Wipplinger sold 75 acres of his farm to the Iowa-Minnesota
Town Site Company in 1899, who divided the land into lots.

This handsome, two story building was Keister's first school house.
The exact date of its construction is unknown.

XVI

On April 6,1865, one Joseph Wing with his wife and daughter, left Antioch Lake County in the state of Illinois to travel west to claim a homestead for his family. On July 14th, 1965, after eight days of travel in a covered wagon, Joseph Wing arrived in Faribault County, Minnesota. He then went to a Seely township where he found a John R. Scisson, the Faribault county surveyor, and had Mr. Scisson mark off his homestead location. That evening, Joseph Wing built a camp around his covered wagon in the center of his property and he and his family started their life in their new home. With this event Joseph Wing became the first settler in the township of Kiester in Faribault County, Minnesota.

One morning in May of 1865 Joseph Wing arose to see smoke rising to the north of his home. He walked to the area and found two families by the name of Conrad in prairie schooners. They too had come from Appleton Wisconsin to claim a homestead in Kiester township. Shortly thereafter, Joseph Wing's two brothers-in-law arrived with their families from Illinois to claim their homestead. This now gave the region five homesteading families and after two more years, in 1867, Kiester Township had twenty-five families and could organize their township and elect town officers.

In 1886 the townspeople erected their first school on 'section 21' of the township, and in 1893 they proudly claimed ownership of a creamery, general store and blacksmith shops. One A.L. Peterson was the buttermaker. The township first blacksmith was one R.R. Hagen.

In 1899 the building of the Iowa, Minnesota and North Western railroad began. The local residents eagerly entered the project with a great deal of enthusiasm. The route of the railroad went from Belle Plains, Iowa, through Mason City to the southeast corner of Kiester township. From there it went to Blue Earth, Fairmont and Fox Lake. The workers laid two and one-half miles of track a day. And the pay was approximately one and one-half dollars a day.

The first paper in Kiester township was called the Kiester Courier. It was an eight page weekly and was first published on February 16, 1890 by the printers of Carpenter and Company.

On December 11, 1900 the townspeople held their first town council meeting. The first council President to be elected was one N.W. Baker and one F.L. Bush was named the town's first recorder. Two days later the council met again to set pay scales for its public servants. The towns's marshall, one Sidney S. Ozmun would receive a salary of fifteen dollars a month and the recorder would receive sixty dollars a year. An ordinance was passed to regulate the sale of intoxicating liquor; it was to be the first ordinance to be passed by the town council. The township began to grow and thrive. The town was situated on an elevated prairie with rolling landscape that provided drainage and was just twenty-one miles from Blue Earth, the county seat. On a clear day many surrounding towns, i.e., Albert Lea, Wells, Thompson and Bricelyn, could be seen from Kiester's hillsides. In 1905 the town population was 500 people.

To raise money the town levied a poll-tax of one and one-half dollars on all males between the ages of twenty-one and fifty years of age. This tax rate was raised to two dollars per male tax-payer six years later. The town was populated by people of Norwegian, Swedish, Irish, English and German descent.

The early settlers had no roads to follow as they moved about the prairie. Wagon tracks served as 'roads'. As more people settled in the area and started farms with definite perimeters, the 'roads' became the area parallel to the perimeters of the farms. Gradually the settlers developed roadbeds and together hauled gravel to cover these early roads. They would decide on a two or three day period and gather to work on hauling gravel. These days would be called 'good roads' or 'graveling days'. All of the males in the area would pitch in to work on the roads while the women and children prepared picnic lunches for the workers.

In 1911 a new creamery was planned and twenty-five new silos were built. The price of farms 'skyrocketed' with one farm of eighty acres being sold for eighty dollars and another for seventy dollars. In November of 1911 the town council met and called a special election. Fifty-eight residents voted in the election to formally separate Kiester village from Kiester township. It would now be a separate tax assessment district. The town had a doctor, dentist and a 'magnetic healer' by 1913. Dr. Urstad was the town doctor and a new hospital was completed. The first birth in the hospital was a baby-boy born to Mr. and Mrs. E.C. Norris.

In 1918 President Wilson declared the end of World War I and there was great rejoicing in the town as eighty of its men had left the town to serve their country.

The village continued to thrive and the 1920 census figures were 729 residents in Kiester township and 257 residents in Kiester Village. The worst fire in the history of Kiester Village was on August 8, 1924 when the Kiester Auto Company burned down destroying the building and thirteen autos in it at the time.

On May 12, 1927 Joseph Wing, Kiester's first settler, died. And on June 1, 1933 Kiester High School had its first graduating senior class.

Tom Haddy, a pioneer in his own right, would move to Kiester and become a force in that town as he had been in Walters.

Scene from a "good roads" or graveling day.

Street scene taken in 1916 Building on the left is Keister Food Market owned by Tom Haddy The old school, the former First National Bank building, and the Keister Hardware Co. building are shown.

XVII

In 1932 in the midst of an economic depression across America Tom opened a store in Kiester, Minnesota as he believed that even with hard economic times he could prosper if he worked hard. He remembered an earlier year when after a year of hard work he and Frances had cried because they had lost $400 dollars in spite of their efforts. But Tom had refused to let those frequent set-backs deter him and he had continued to strive for success. Kiester was seven miles from Walters. Two years earlier John Michael Haddy, son of Uncle Mike Assaf El Haddy, of Cedar Rapids, Iowa; the same Uncle Mike that had taken Tom in on his arrival in America, came to work for Tom. John was born on May 1, 1912 in Cedar Rapids. When Tom opened the store in Kiester, John's brother Sam moved from Cedar Rapids to run the Kiester store for Tom. By involving members of other branches of his family Tom was acting in keeping with the philosophy of the small village of Ain Arab where villagers worked together to help and support one another and to include members of the family in their prosperity.

One year later, on August 6, 1933 John Haddy married Tom's oldest daughter Elizabeth in Cedar Rapids, Iowa. They took over the running of the Walter's store and Tom and Frances with their other six children moved to Kiester to run that store. In 1934 John and Elizabeth bought the Walters store from Tom.

The family now owned three stores, one in Conger run by Joe Shaheen, Frances' father, one in Kiester run by Tom and one in Walters run by Elizabeth and John. Their slogan was "Three good stores in three good towns" but all of the stores ran as one and shared resources. They borrowed money to expand and bought a truck which was used to deliver groceries. The idea of having movies for the farmers and their families to watch when they came to town on Saturday night was expanded so that all three stores sponsored these movies. Roy Beamsley ran the movies and each small town had a different night for the movies.

The Kiester store was on a street corner on the main street of town and had a front and side entrance. The side entrance opened on a back room that was used for receiving eggs. Show nights, including Saturday night, were the busiest times of the week. The farmers would drive up to the side entrance, deliver their fifteen or thirty dozen cases of eggs to the back room, go to the front and leave their grocery list and then go outside to watch the free movie featuring Tom Mix or Hoot Gibson.

During the movies the Haddy clan candled eggs, a process of shining a light through the egg to see if any of them were rotten. Francis worked in the back room. Joe worked up in the front of the store and wore a white apron and also worked in the back with Francis. It was necessary to move fast or the cases of eggs piled up. Francis was good at candling, grading and counting the eggs. He lifted the layers out of the cases without breaking them and when he accidently broke some eggs Joe would scold him. Francis, to get rid of Joe's nagging, would tell Joe that one of his girlfriends was in the front of the store. And Joe, who had lots of girlfriends, would take the bait and hustle back to the front of the store.

One day, Francis decided to write his name and address on an egg wondering where it would land. The eggs and poultry were delivered to the larger markets of the cities in southern Minnesota for distribution. The egg with Francis' name on it was shipped to New York. A young man in New York who received the egg, thought that Francis was a girl and wrote to him. Francis then sent the young man a picture of one of sisters and the boy sent his picture back. When the local paper, The Kiester Courier published the story Francis, thinking that things were getting out of hand, hastily stopped writing to the boy.

They had a large truck and a pick-up truck and all groceries for the three stores were bought in Albert Lea so that they could buy in bulk and get discounted prices. They met once a week to plan for the weeks specials which were put into a bulletin and sent to the farmers in the farming areas nearby. They built an excellent credit reputation with all of the suppliers for groceries and dry goods as they paid their bills promptly and on time.

As he had done in Walters, Tom became involved in the life of the town of Kiester, for he still believed that his success depended on his becoming active in the affairs of the towns where his customers lived. In Kiester, Tom, with five other men and Mr. Talle, the banker, built a theater. As with any large lusty family there many moments of humor in their daily lives. One day, young Francis went with his father in their red ford pick-up truck to pick up some chickens from a nearby farmer. Their routine was to go at night so that the chickens, which the farmer was keeping loose in a grove of trees, would be easier to capture as they roosted and slept in the tree limbs. Tom had a chicken coop in the back of the truck and as they captured the chickens by plucking them from the tree limbs as they slept, they would put them into the chicken coop in the back of the truck. Francis made a mistake and left the chicken coop door open. The aroused chickens squawked and clucked in irritation at having their sleep disturbed and scrambled and fluttered away from the coop back into the grove. Tom, his upset son and the farmer spent the next few hours chasing and recapturing the scattered and squawking chickens to put them back into the coop.

The familial bond that was created by working together created a sense of harmony and well being so that the family members and extended family members became close and presented a solid front to their competitors.

XVIII

The years slipped by and Tom and Frances and their children were living pleasant, active and enriching lives. It was fall of the year 1940 and his children were fast becoming adults. Tom sat in a chair and thought about Francis, his second son. He thought back on the day the year before when Francis had told him that he wanted to go to college. Tom had been startled at his son's request, as he had hoped that his sons and daughters would join him in his successful business for which he had worked so hard. When he and Frances had discussed Francis' request, she had told Tom that he had best let young Francis decide for himself what his future would be, and she pointed out that Francis said he would like to try to get into medical school and to pursue a career in Medicine. Tom had been torn between the pride that he felt that one of his sons wished to become a doctor and his fear that he would lose his beloved children to work of which he knew very little. The pangs of fear of the effects of his children having minds of their own and of their Americanized views had set in. Tom had reluctantly agreed that Francis could go to college and Francis had enrolled at Luther College, in Decorah, Iowa and was a freshman there.

Tom sat and reread Francis' first letter home after having left them a few days before. He read and reread Francis' letter as he coped with the sense of loss that he felt at the his son's going away from the family.

'Dear Folks,

After my first day at college I find that I am really satisfied, and boy, was it ever a big and full day.

At 10:00 this morning we went to chapel and listened to speeches on 'How to fit into your environment' and then after that we took an English Placement test. It wasn't so bad. In the afternoon we went to Chapel again and were formerly introduced to the faculty. Speroti, the band director, is really a great old guy. He's hard of hearing but he has got so much wit for an old man

that he had us laying in the aisles from laughter. Tonight, we had
a mixer party where faculty members and students met in the gym
and we were entertained by singers, speakers etc. Then each one
got a partner for a grand march. (This was to get the students
acquainted with one another). A lunch was served afterwards.
Percing came today. We've got the rooms changed around .
    Its getting late and I'm going to bed.

Good night
Collegian
I'm not homesick yet'

XIX

The year was 1941, Tom was listening to the radio. The war in Europe was getting worse and most people thought that it would only be a matter of time before the United States would enter the fray. Tom thought back to the years when he was young and all of the young Lebanese men were being put into the Turkish Army. He realized that by coming to America when he was eighteen years old he had escaped being forced to served in the army of a foreign country. But, this war would be a war that his sons would become involved in. America was now his country and his children's country and if America became involved in a war his sons' duty would be to serve their country.

As everyone expected the United States was faced with going to war. On December 7, 1941 the Japanese carried out a surprise attack on Pearl Harbor in Hawaii. President Roosevelt declared war on Japan and was planning to declare war on Germany as well.

Joe would enlist in the Army and go into the anti-tank corps. Francis also registered but received a deferment as he was headed for medical school.

Tom sat in a chair and thought about his son Francis' plans to go to medical school. He had applied to the University of Minnesota's School of Medicine and needed letters of recommendation from members of the community who knew the young man well. Tom thought, "I will ask my good friend Mr. Talle the banker, to write for Francis." Mr. Talle said that he would be delighted to write in support of Francis' entering medical school. And in the year 1943 Francis became a freshman at the University of Minnesota' s School of Medicine and with the rest of his medical school classmates was inducted into a branch of the service, the Army's Specialized Training Program. Because of the war students did not take summers off and went to school year-round to speed up finishing their education. The uncertainty of the times created a sense of urgency to finish as much as possible of one's peace-time activities before the war and its demands on the people of the United States pushed all other plans aside. The speed-up for medical students was mandated by the United States Government, which saw that there would be an increased need for physicians as a result of the war.

It was July of 1942 and Tom was celebrating his fiftieth birthday. Joe had entered the Army in March of this year and had been selected for Officer's Candidate School and had graduated as an army Lieutenant. Tom was very proud of his son's achievement and prayed that the good Lord would watch over his oldest son and bring him back safely from this terrible war. He missed his children very much as he held a letter in his hand from Francis that filled him with joy. He reread it slowly so that he could savor every word on the paper. It said:

'Dear Dad,
Buying a present for a father is difficult and sending a card is inadequate so I've decided that writing a letter especially to you would come closer to filling the requirements than anything else. I was listening to a father's day radio program today and it brought back a lot of pleasant memories about you and I. Believe me Dad, I realize what a fine guy you are and I miss your presence a lot. I realize also just how much you have given me, not only in material things but in advice, guidance and insight into little problems a guy meets everyday. Remember the time I took the red pickup without asking (and against your orders) and drove to a show in Wells with a couple of the boys. On the way back I had a pretty bad accident. I was really scared of what you were going to say and what you should have said, but what happened? You told me to not let it happen again, to take that as a lesson and said you were happy that we were all right. You weren't even sore. It's things like that that I remember-and appreciate. That's what I mean when I say you're a fine guy. Remember the day I left for college. You and I sat down on the corner of the kitchen table-the corner nearest the door- and we had a little talk. I remember all of it Dad. You told me about the time you left your father, the little talk you had. You said you thought that that day was the last I'll really be home for good- you told me to be a good guy. I've tried to be a good guy. Then there was the time you caught Joe and I

smoking cigarette butts we picked up off the street. What you did that day was one of the wisest things I think any father has ever done. We had a little talk. You didn't give us a beating-which we no doubt deserved. You told us that if we wanted to smoke, the store was full of good clean cigarettes, that we should smoke in front of you and not behind your back and that it didn't make a bit of difference to you. I didn't touch a cigarette from that day until I was a sophomore in college. You really used psychology. Remember when you tried making a lefty pitcher out of me. I didn't do so well but I'll never forget your trying as long as I live. And the time my high school love was having a party and I didn't have any pants. I was a sophomore then. I told you about it and you dam near laughed your head off. You had Joe make a special trip to Bricyln to buy me a pair of trousers. It seems like the little things are the important happenings-anyway they're the things I remember and appreciate most. How about the time I was making my gas model airplane and everyone else thought putting all that money into a motor was downright silly. You didn't. I remember that talk we had. It ended up with your buying it for me. And the time I made the mistake on my medical school application and was turned down. Remember what you said. You told me that something must have been wrong and that I'd soon get in. And two weeks later I did. Just the other day you sent me a $25 check just to celebrate with because of my marks. It wasn't necessary to do that but you sent it anyway. Thanks a lot Dad.
All my love
Francis

Tom felt a warm glow as he read Francis' letter and realized that the Lebanese belief that family members are always bound together no matter how far apart they may be was very true. Traditionally Lebanese emigrants rarely sever ties with the village of their birth. In the native village the emigrant is still thought of as a member of the village even if they have been gone for fifty or sixty years. Most Lebanese families are based on the patriarchal idea of patrilineal descent. Social standards are maintained by family members. Familial relationships are maintained across long distances, across countries and across the world.

The family gives protection, support and opportunity to its

members and its members give back loyalty, love and service. The family is the basis of the Lebanese culture and the religion to which one belongs is, to a degree, like an extended family of the individual. It is assumed that an individual will always give allegiance to his family or kin first and foremost. Family members are concerned for each other and give aid to one another. The classic form of the family is the generational patrilineal extended family. Man and wife, their children, their sons and daughters families. This cultural philosophy creates a strong sense of shared identity.

XX

The changes in the Haddy family's lives were coming quickly. Frances began to complain of fatigue and was losing weight. Although she did not voice her concerns to Tom she worried that the family was splitting up and she feared that in the process she would lose her children to the outside world. She worried that her daughters, who were now of marriageable age would not find suitable men of the Lebanese background in this midwestern part of the country. For deep within her Frances cherished the idea that her children would marry others of the Lebanese heritage and carry on that ethnic culture. She recognized that she and Tom had raised seven young Americans but she clung to the hope that they would marry other LebaneseAmericans and that their ethnic heritage would remain intact. She was facing the age-old pain that immigrants faced when it became apparent that their children would move away from the ethnic culture of their parents and become a blend of their inherited culture and the culture to which they were exposed in their formative and growing years. The immigrant parents were torn between the wish for their children to have a better life than that from which they had fled and which had brought them to America and the sense of loss that they felt when their children grew to be different from them. The fears and uncertainties that these immigrant parents felt were deep-rooted and difficult for their children to understand. The parents saw the movement of their children away from their heritage as a form of rejection and loss and their children saw their parents dogged determination to keep their ethnic heritage intact as old-fashioned and an infringement on their independence. The sharp contrast of views led to many harsh and angry confrontations in the immigrant families as it would in Tom and Frances' family.

Because she complained of not feeling well Tom took her to a local doctor who could not pinpoint the problem and suggested to Tom that he take her to the Mayo Clinic for evaluation. Tom was told that Frances' health would improve if she moved to a warmer climate as the harsh Minnesota winters were difficult for her to cope with as she aged.

The second world war had depleted the help that Tom needed for running the stores, Tom's son-in-law John Haddy in the Walters store had entered the Navy, his brother-in-law George Shaheen in the Conger store had entered the Marines, and his two boys Joe and Francis were gone. Like all young Americans they were all setting aside their personal lives to volunteer to serve their country. Their absence and the fact that his wife became ill, caused Tom to decide to make a move to a warmer climate.

Tom decided to sell the store in Kiester and move to California. So after building a career in general merchandising from 1916 to 1943 in southern Minnesota Tom moved to California in the year of 1943 arriving on September 9th with Juanita and Vernita. Joe was in the Army and Francis was also in the Army as a medical student assigned to the ASTP program at the University of Minnesota's School of Medicine. Beatrice and Lucille were already living in California as they had gone there for jobs. The outbreak of the war had created many good-paying jobs throughout the country and people from all parts of the country were moving to take advantage of the opportunities that were created.

The separation of the family members was painful for Tom and Frances but they realized that their children were adults and reaffirmed their faith that in the Lebanese culture, family members were together no matter how far apart they were physically. And just as the Lebanese believed that no immigrant ever severs his ties with his home village no family member severs his ties with his family.

Tom, Frances and the girls took several weeks to make the trip to their new home in California as they took the opportunity to stop and visit the many relatives that they had in Cedar Rapids, Iowa and in other towns throughout the Southwest. Tom arrived in Los Angeles, California on September 29, 1943 and immediately contacted other Lebanese-Americans in the area and settled his family in a house at 3722 Tracy Street in Hollywood.

Tom was looking for an opportunity to buy a produce market in Hollywood and spent a great deal of time talking to prospective sellers and other merchants in the area so that he could make a wise decision. There were several businesses for sale as many young men had left their businesses to serve in the war effort. He took his time in deciding on a store to buy and worked in the May Department store in the men's department where he quickly rose to being the manager of the department. But a grocery store to buy was what he was looking for and he decided on a grocery store located on Fountain Street and Sunset Boulevard. As he had in Walters and Kiester Minnesota he soon had a thriving grocery store in operation. Frances was at his side as before but Tom hoped that when this war that the country was fighting was over his family would return and continue in the grocery business and that the Haddys could pick up the threads of their lives.

But Tom's hopes for serenity and family adhesiveness was not to be. One year later Joe wrote to tell his family that he had married Erma Rae Garrett on August 12, 1944 in Llano, Texas. Erma Rae Garrett had been born on February 18, 1924 in San Saba, Texas and she was not of Lebanese descent. Frances reacted badly. Her fears were becoming a reality. Her children would be breaking away from their heritage and the family solidarity that she so desperately wanted would not be. Tom tried to soften her disappointment by telling her that it was inevitable that some of their children would marry nonLebanese but that did not mean that the family would not continue to be strong. But, Frances' convictions were deep rooted and she could not accept this marriage.

This first major break from what Frances perceived as the family's solidarity would cause Frances many hours of despair and heartache but she would eventually accept the fact that her children were Americans and would be influenced by that culture as much as they would be by the Lebanese heritage that she so deeply felt. She would accept that the melding of cultures that took place in America was a part of her children's heritage also and that they still would feel deeply their parents heritage that had been passed on to them.

Soon after his marriage Joe brought his new bride home to his family. Frances and Tom held a reception for Joe and Rae and proudly presented the new couple to their extended family and friends. Joe was then shipped overseas as part of the First Army to fight in Germany. He fought in the Battle of the Bulge as a tank destroyer leader with six tank destroyers and sixty men under his command. He earned the purple heart and silver star for bravery and in 1945 he was promoted to Captain. On Victory Day Joe was stationed in Czechoslovakia. It was the springtime of the year and Joe was serving as a burgermeister of a small town that was receiving prisoners, captured vehicles and captured champagne, beer and cognac. The men under his command had stripped off their uniforms and were splashing in a nearby stream where they were cooling the captured beer. Joe was also half dressed with no shirt on and unshaven when General George Patton arrived. The General reprimanded Joe when he found out that he was in command and suggested that Joe should be court-marshalled. However, Joe's immediate commanding officer thought that with Joe's superb war record, to court-martial him at the end of the war would be ridiculous and did not follow General Patton's request.

XXI

The war years were passing and the United States with its allies was achieving success on all of the battlefronts. The radio and newspapers reported every day that the enemies of Germany, Japan and their allies were being defeated on all fronts.

On October 25,1944 Tom's daughter Vernita married a Eugene Sam Haddy of Cedar Rapids, Iowa. Eugene was born on February 21, 1921 in Cedar Rapids, Iowa and worked in a grocery business with his father until the beginning of World War II. Eugene then went into the Navy and attended Officers' Candidate School of Aviation and graduated with the rank of Lieutenant. He flew coast guard planes from California to Japan and at the end of the war, when discharged, went back to Cedar Rapids, Iowa to run a grocery store. Later he would buy a restaurant and supper club called the Flame Room.

Frances was pleased that her daughters were marrying men with a Lebanese background and some of her fears were lessened. On February 7, 1945 Tom's beloved daughter Beatrice married one Wadiea Joseph Abraham of Joice, Iowa. Tom was pleased at this new addition to the family. Wadiea, whom everyone called Tony, had been born on January 8, 1910 in Cedar Rapids, Iowa. In 1942 he had enlisted in the Army, been promoted to sergeant, and in 1944 he had been wounded and had been decorated for bravery in the service of his country. The young couple were married in Hollywood, California. Frances was delighted that her second daughter was marrying another Lebanese. Before the war, Wadeia had worked in a general merchandising store that his father owned in Joice, Iowa and after the war the young couple returned to Joice where Tony ran a grocery store with his brother.

The war ended and on August 15, 1945 a Victory Day was celebrated by tired but happy Americans who were grateful for the end to the long four years that their loved ones had been separated from them.

Tom sat and said a prayer of thanks to his God that his loved ones were safe and would be soon returning home. He decided that to celebrate this Victory Day of his adopted country he would write a letter to his children. And so he wrote--

'To our children and loved ones,

This morning on this day of victory, August 15, 1945, the first morning since December 7, 1941, we woke up looking out the window gazing at the beautiful sun. Yes, she too was smiling peacefully. It was a different looking sun, a different looking day. To us it was a brighter sun, more shining and joyful. Our hearts smile too, with joy and happiness to think that all of us now can smile and truly smile right deep from our hearts instead of laughing and trying to forget our worries and troubles.

In nearly all the past four years we tried to put on and tried to forget but... we could not forget ever. If we were at a gathering or at any entertainment, our minds were always with our children and loved one away from us. They may be uncomfortable or they may be in danger. We may never see them again. Yes those thoughts always bothered us. For the past four years there was no joy for us. Our hearts were heavy, our mind was filled with worry.

But this morning it was different. The heavy load is off, our minds are cleared up. We can smile deeply from our hearts. The whole world is smiling. The sun is much brighter and telling us that there is peace on earth again. Our prayers were answered... God was good to us. We never can thank Him enough for his mercy in guiding every one of our children and loved ones. We must not forget Him. He is the one that gave us the Victory over our ruthless enemy. He is the one that gave us the will and power and the brain to accomplish and produce the Atomic bomb before our enemy. With his will and power, we had it first. It would have been just too bad for the whole world if the enemy had gotten it first. Now the world is safe and that was his will. Let us say "God always bless America. America is the back-bone of a every peace-loving country"

How wonderful it is now to think that our children and loved ones will soon be coming home again, home safe and sound. How wonderful it is to start plans for the future without any fear in the hearts of everyone. Yes, we are born again. The world is a new world now and let us look for brighter prospects in the future. Let us not think of the dark days past and ponder over it. Your futures are the thing we must think of now.

With the Lord's help and blessing we will go ahead again, Amen.

With a joyful heart, we sit down quietly on this Victory Day and write these words to all of you. For this day we have waited a long time so we can we can see you all soon and be together again. Home to stay and home to prosperity and home to enjoy home and live in peace. Now we are all resting, the heavy load is off, and we are waiting for you all to come home again. God be with you all always.

Mom and Dad '

XXII

The war was over and Tom was grateful to his God that his son's and sons-in-law had returned from the war safely. He was hopeful that these young men would return home and the family would continue in the retail merchandise store business that he had spent so many years learning in Minnesota. He would be pleasantly surprised in the next few years at how many of his family members chose to become merchants as he had so many years ago when he had come to the United States and had become a merchant himself.

In 1946 Tom's oldest son Joe returned from serving his country and he and his wife Rae came to Los Angeles to live. Joe, George Shaheen, Frances' brother and John Haddy, Elizabeth's husband bought a grocery store on North Vermont Street in Hollywood. This grocery store would cater to what was known as the Los Feliz trade with notables as W.C. Fields, Jack Dempsey, and Raymond Burr as their customers.

The year 1946 was to be a memorable one for Tom. His oldest daughter Elizabeth who was married to John Haddy was coming back to Hollywood, California at the war's end. John had enlisted in the Navy in 1942 and had served his country until 1945. During his service years Elizabeth had followed John from one assignment to another in order to be close to where John was until he was shipped overseas. And now they were coming back to Hollywood to be close to the family. In April of 1946 Tom's younger son, Francis graduated from the University of Minnesota's School of Medicine at the age of twenty-three. Tom felt a surge of pride at his son's accomplishment. One of his children had succeeded in getting a professional education. And as any immigrant he was grateful for the opportunity to have raised his children in this wonderful land of America.

On August 4, 1946 Joe became the proud father of a baby girl that he and Rae named Sharon Jo and Tom was a proud grandfather for the first time. Sharon was born in Hollywood, California. The next generation of

Haddys had started.

In the memorable year of 1946 Tom would receive a letter telling him that his beloved father, Joseph, had died. Before he had died Joseph had built his own grave of rock. As he read the letter over and over Tom wept with grief at the loss of the strong and beautiful man who had been his father. The man who had taught him so much about life and who had been responsible for what Tom had become. He thought back to the day when he had left his parents to come to America and how he had looked back on his grieving parents sitting on a rock as he walked away from them. He thought of the thought that had passed through his mind at that time, that his father was thinking that he would never see Tom again and his father's fears had been realized. He had died without ever seeing his eldest son again. Tom berated himself for not having gone back to see his parents during the years since he had left and although he realized that he had been very busy working to raise and care for his family it was not a good enough reason to have not made the trip back to visit. He grieved for his loss and for the anguished guilt that he felt.

Francis had been writing that he was interested in marrying a girl who was a fellow-classmate of his and another painful time for Frances and Tom occurred as the girl that their second son wished to marry was not of Lebanese descent but of German descent. Frances again found it difficult to accept the fact that her sons were marrying women who were not of their culture. She anguished over this and her disapproval of her sons choices for wives caused severe strains in the family's relations. Like most immigrants to this land, she saw her children marrying individuals of other cultures as a rejection of the family heritage. Of course, the melding of different ethnic groups in America had been occurring from the founding of this country and was indeed the foundation of her strength and diversity. However, Frances did not think in these terms but rather in her fierce desire to keep the family ethnically intact into the future generations. She would adjust to a degree to this mixing of cultures within her family but she would never completely accept this aspect of being a member of an ethnically diverse land such as America.

But, the Americanization of Tom's children continued and on September 21, 1946 Francis married Theresa Brey who had been born on February 27, 1924 in Wabasso, Minnesota, the daughter of a country doctor. Another of the pioneers who had made America what she was, the country doctor who practiced medicine under the most difficult circumstances, serving the country people of the farmlands of Minnesota with a minimum of supplies and facilities. Truly practicing the art of medicine rather than just the science of it.

On September 26, 1946 in Cedar Rapids, Iowa, Tom's beloved daughter Vernita and her husband Eugene became the parents of a girl that they named Bonnie Jean and Tom had his second grandchild. The Haddy clan was expanding and Tom was delighted.

On November 12, 1946 his growing brood of grandchildren was increased when his daughter Beatrice and her husband Tony, who were living in Joice, Iowa, became parents of a son that they named Thomas Joseph. Tom was delighted at the birth of his first grandson and namesake.

And also in this year of 1946 Tom was invited to a meeting that was held in the Mode-O-Day building on Washington street in Los Angeles where a group of Lebanese-Americans came to the decision that they would build a cathedral for the Orthodox parishioners in the Los Angeles areas. In attending this meeting Tom was starting another major event of his life. This proposed church would give Tom the opportunity to help plan, create and support an orthodox church for his fellow Lebanese to attend. This church would become the focus of their lives and provide the inspirational support for their daily living. Tom was very excited at the prospect of being involved in this undertaking.

XXIII

Like most ethnic groups who had migrated to America, Americans of Arabic descent were becoming an important contributing group in the land that their parents had adopted. In 1947 a group of exservicemen who had served in all branches of the service during the second world war petitioned the American Legion in Los Angeles for a charter. The request was granted in 1948 and the new post was named the John Gantus Post #792. Master Sergeant John Gantus had been the first Californian of Arabic heritage who had lost his life in the service of his country during World War II. All members of this post were veterans of Arabic descent. In 1951, the wives and mothers of these veterans would form the ladies auxiliary of the post. As they had given their service to the United States of America during the war, these men and their wives and mothers continued their service to America by making the focus of the John Gantus Post of the American Legion service to others.

They gave service of time and money to the Veterans Hospital at Sautelle, and the Children's Orthopedic Shrine Hospital. They helped the less-fortunate families of the surrounding area.

George Haddy was a member of the group and he had become Tom's son-in-law on January 12, 1947 when Tom's beloved daughter Lucille had married him. George worked for Tom in his store. George was born on December 27, 1919 in Scarville, Iowa the son of Mike Abusomra Haddy. He had enlisted in the Air Force's parachute troops during the second world war and had been wounded and decorated for bravery during the battle of the bulge. Tom was very proud of the honorable men that his daughters were marrying.

In 1947 Francis, Tom's son, went to Panama to serve as an Army Air Force doctor as part of his commitment to the Government to serve in repayment for his medical education.

XXIV

This year of 1947 would be another memorable one for Tom as he was busily preparing to take his wife and daughter Juanita back to Lebanon for a visit. Learning of his father's death the year before had shaken Tom because he had not returned for a visit before his father's death in all the years that he had been separated from his parents. He had decided that he would go back and see his mother before she too would be lost to him.

The date of their departure was August 6, 1947 and on the evening of August 5, 1947 their many friends and relatives gathered at their home to say good-bye to Tom, Frances and Juanita as they spent their last night before leaving. It was a happy and excited group, as whenever members of the American-Lebanese community returned to the mother-land for a visit, many others wanted them to convey their greetings to their relatives back in Lebanon.

Early on August 6, 1947 Tom and his wife and daughter rose early, gathered their luggage and went to Joe's home to once more say good-bye, then they stopped at the market that they owned and said good-bye to Lucille and George as they made their way to the train station. Frances' sister Selma and several other friends accompanied them to the train station.

At 11:30 a.m. the train left Los Angeles for Cedar Rapids, Iowa where the travelers would visit with more relatives and friends before going on to New York to board the ship that would take them to Lebanon. The train was delayed but arrived in Cedar Rapids on the morning of August 8, 1947. Beatrice and Vernita met their parents and sister as the train arrived and brought their babies, Tommy and Bonnie, to see their grandparents.

Tom, Frances and Juanita stayed in Cedar Rapids for two nights visiting relatives. The forty-eight hours that they spent there were filled with eating, drinking and enjoying being with their daughters and their families and their extended family of relatives. The closeness of the extended family, that is a part of the Lebanese culture, made these visits an event of warm and loving relationships. And on the morning of August 11, 1947 the travelers reboarded the train and continued their journey back to the land of their roots.

In Cedar Rapids, Tom and his family were joined by a Mr. and Mrs. Alex Nimmer, who lived in Mexico, and who were also making the trip back to Lebanon for a visit. They spoke no English and Frances acted as interpreter for them and her daughter Juanita who spoke no Arabic. Juanita would learn many words of the Lebanese language before she arrived in Lebanon. The weather was extremely hot and the air-conditioning on the train did not work, so the travelers became hot and uncomfortable but the excitement of their journey kept them in good spirits. They arrived in Chicago at 3:30 on August 11, 1947 for the next leg of their journey. At 5:00 a.m. the next morning the train left Chicago and headed for New York where Tom and his family would board the ship that would take them back to Lebanon. He was nervous but elated at the prospect of returning to his homeland and a sadness filled his heart in knowing that his beloved father would not be there to greet him. When their train arrived in New York at 9:30 p.m. they went to their hotel where they met others who were making the trip to their homeland. Frances and Juanita were fascinated by the sights and sounds of New York. They had never been there and it was so different from Los Angeles. The next morning Tom, Frances and Juanita took the subway to Washington Street where many Lebanese immigrant families lived. Lebanese people are 'family' to other Lebanese no matter where they go and the Haddys were soon enjoying themselves meeting and talking to others of their heritage.

They then took a cab to see the sights of New York, they drove through Wall Street, saw the Empire State Building and went to Radio City Music Hall that evening to see a show. They were elated at the experience of seeing the fascinating city of New York.

On the 15th of August they left their hotel room and went to the docks to board the ship that would take them to Lebanon. The ship belonged to the Marin Corporation and they boarded at 9:30 a.m. The ship that they boarded was a refitted war transport ship and the first to be used for commercial sailing after the war. After going through customs they found their cabin on the third deck. There were 24 beds in the room. The room was clean and there was another room for baths and showers. Their food was served cafeteria style. Their departure from New York was delayed as the ships workers were on strike but the ship did finally leave New York at 8:30 p.m. They remained on the deck until 9:30 as the ship left the New York harbor and then went to their cabin to sleep. The men and women had separate quarters. The next morning the ship's bell called them to breakfast and as they were going to the cafeteria, they noticed that the ship's crew and staff were wearing life jackets. They found out that someone had thrown a cigarette from the upper deck and it had started a fire. The fire was quickly put out and they continued to their breakfast. Frances was seasick and did not want to eat but Tom and Juanita urged her to try to eat something. She did so and immediately became sick to her stomach. They were then called to an emergency drill practice on the ship's deck by the ship's staff and they all went onto the deck to practice the emergency drill.

The days of the sea voyage took on a routine of meals, visiting with and getting to know the other passengers, playing cards and in the evenings dancing on the deck. Some of the days were very hot and the passengers stayed below the top deck to seek a cool spot. There were several days of rain and these served to cool the air and provide the passengers with a measure of relief from the heat of the hot sun. Frances suffered many days from sea-sickness and often would skip meals. For several days the sea was rough and the ship's decks swayed with the unevenness of the oceans' s surface. On these days the passengers who were bothered by motion sickness stayed in their bunks and waited for the sea to become calm once more.

Tom sat on a deck chair and thought back thirty-seven years to his first trip across this vast ocean called the Atlantic. The long years in between had been two-thirds of his life, he had a family of seven children and had been a success in his caring for and providing for his family. His children were all married except Juanita and were raising families of their own and the next generation of Haddys was well on its way to being established. Only now, the generations were Americans and their parents were taking their place as members of the vast and diverse society known as the people of the United States of America. He felt very proud of his family and looked forward to being a part of their lives and the lives of their children, his beloved grandchildren. It was so true that no matter where people of the Lebanese heritage lived or were born they would carry on the traditions of their culture. The children would not only be Americans, as his children were, but would also be part of the children of intermarriages with others of different cultures whose parents or ancestors had been immigrants to America as he was. America was indeed a melting pot of heritages and cultures. And his family was a part of that melding.

After eight days at sea they passed Gibralter in the middle of the night and did not see that impressive sight. The sea was rough here but soon became calmer as they sailed on into the Mediterranean. The trip became interesting as they saw the mountains, fish and birds who had flown out to sea from the nearby land masses and many ships that passed them along their route. The other ships signaled them with their foghorns and their ship answered the salute. The passing of other ships during the night was exceptionally beautiful as their many lights shone brightly against the darkened sky.

The passengers became more lively and eager as the end of their long journey was near. Four days later, they saw Beirut harbor and knew that their journey was at an end. As the ship neared the dock Tom saw his mother, his brothers, sister and other family members waiting for them. He became very excited and saddened as he watched them waiting for him. The long years of separation from his beloved family were coming to an end.

As Tom descended the stairs to the dock he and his mother fell into each others arms and the tears flowed profusely. Tom's brothers and sister crowded around and the next fifteen minutes was filled with hugs and kisses that had been saved for years during their separation. The family then went to a hotel in Beirut where rooms had been reserved for Tom and his family. There, they met more relatives who had come to Beirut to welcome them. Tom had been told that he could not get his trunks off of the ship until several days later so his Lebanese family went shopping and bought Tom, Frances and Juanita clothes and toiletries to tide them over until they could get their trunks with most of their belongings. The clan celebrated the reunion in Beirut and waited until the trunks in the ship's hold were available for them to pick up.

The next morning Tom, Frances, Juanita, Tom's family and their friends filled a bus for the trip to Ain Arab from Beirut. As they left the city and started to travel through the countryside Tom and Frances enjoyed the beauty of the countryside that was their homeland. Juanita was impressed at the beauty of the land from which her parents had come. The people gathered in the bus started to sing in pure joy at having one of their own return for a visit. Tom and Frances wept at the love that surrounded them. When they got to within two miles of Ain Arab there was a group of the town's children waiting for them. The bus stopped to pick them up and the singing went on. As they entered the town the townspeople poured into the street shouting, singing and shooting off their guns to welcome the Haddys. The town's main street was nothing more that stones and dirt and Tom was amazed that he had forgotten how poor this town was. As they went into his mother's house Tom greeted all of the townspeople that had gathered at the door. They started to tell Tom and Frances what their names were and who they were. It was difficult to remember all of their names and how they were related or how they were friends of Tom's family.

Tom took his mother's hand and asked her to walk with him to his father's grave. They walked to a hillside where Joseph had built a tomb for his burial. Tom knelt at his father's gravesite and wept uncontrollably. The grief that had been with him since he had heard of his father's death the year before washed over him and he prayed and wept at the loss of his beloved father. His mother knelt beside him and wept with him. Tom stayed at his father's gravesite as the memories of his early childhood and Joseph's words flooded through his mind. The pain of not having seen his father once more before his death would stay with Tom for the rest of his life.

For the next several days the visitors poured into the small house in which Tom had grown up. There was food, laughter, tears and singing. Many of them had relatives in America and although they were unknown to Tom there was always the hope that he might know of their family members who lived in America.

A band of gypsies came into town and danced, sang and played their guitars. The whole town turned out for the festivities. Tom, Frances and Juanita were overwhelmed with the attention that they received.

On the eighth of September, Tom, his family and several of the townspeople took a bus to Damascus on their way to Sedneya where the ancient church healing shrine of St. Mary's Cathedral was located. The church had been built on the top of a steep hill and the visitors walked up many flights of steps to the cathedral. As they entered they saw the beautiful and ancient chandeliers of the church. The church was filled with worshipers from miles around. Many had come here looking for healing of their bodies and their spirits. The cathedral was known for miles around as a place where miracles of healing took place. It drew, like a magnet, those many people whose lives were troubled by ill health, family discord or poverty. When they left the cathedral many felt a new sense of hope and well-being. As in so many parts of the world where poverty and poor health were present, the church provided the solace so desperately needed by those who lived in these conditions.

The Haddys and their relatives returned to Ain Arab after stopping, once again, in Damascus and seeing more of that city. The next several days were filled with more visits by friends and relatives who spent the days and evenings, eating, talking and dancing. Frances, who was not used to such ongoing activity often was weary before going to bed, but she knew how much this visit meant to Tom and she was cheerful and pleasant to all who came to visit at her mother-in-law's home.

Tom and Frances had been approached by a local dentist, Dr. Elias Nemer who asked for Juanita's hand in marriage. They were dismayed as they realized that the young man was following the custom of his homeland and did not understand that in America, young women picked their own mates and the custom of parents arranging marriages for their children was not an American custom. They spoke to Juanita of the young man's request and she told them that she did not know this Elias Nemer and could not marry him. Tom and Frances then tried to very gently tell the young man that Juanita was not interested in marrying him and that the custom's of America and Lebanon were not the same. He was disappointed but told them that he understood.

On the 17th of September the Haddy's and some of Tom's relatives went to Beirut to visit the American Consulate. They could not see the consulate that day so they decided to stay overnight in Beruit and visit some of the historic sights of that city. They visited the St. George's church, which was three-hundred years old. And also visited the castle of the Amir Basheer which was one-hundred and fifty years old. It had taken one thousand men twenty years to build the castle for the Amir. They enjoyed a pleasant day sight-seeing in Beirut and then returned to Ain Arab by bus.

The days of their visit passed with visits from friends and relatives of both Tom and Frances who were back in the country where they were born. Each visit was a celebration as two members of the homeland were back. Side trips to nearby towns were made to visit other friends and relatives and Frances found the pace of all of the socializing tiring.

Tom's brother Elias was planning to marry and Tom and Frances were soon caught up in helping him to prepare for his wedding. His intended bride, Sarah Azam, lived in the small town of Meimas, a nearby town and there were many trips to be made back and forth for the many wedding preparations. Frances found herself making the dresses for the bride and for her mother-in-law and sister-in-law. She was an accomplished seamstress and made the dresses for the women of the family quickly. The town of Meimas' population was three-quarters Muslim and their cultural traditions flavored the wedding plans of Elias. His future bride, Sarah, and he like any young couple were nervous and excited over their coming marriage and like most young couples were planning for their future with a high degree of optimism. There were many trips between the two towns of the couples and many discussions and plans for the wedding.

Tom, Frances, Juanita, Tom's mother, sisters, brothers and a group of friends from the town went to Meimas to escort the bride back to Ain Arab for the wedding. As they arrived the streets of Meimas were crowded with people who had come out to welcome the group from Ain Arab. There was singing, dancing in the streets, and much talk as everyone was excited at the marriage of Elias and Sarah. The group from Ain Arab, partied and visited with the townspeople of Meimas throughout the day. It seemed to Frances that everyone in the town was visiting the bride-to-be. The bride's home was jammed with people and Frances struggled to do the last minute fittings for the bride's clothes. After several hours of visiting, Tom and Frances went to bed to try to get some rest before the wedding day. The next morning, Sarah, her family and a large group of townspeople joined the Ain Arab group in returning to Ain Arab for the wedding. It was Sunday and Elias and Sarah's wedding day. As the caravan of cars and buses approached Ain Arab the townspeople poured into the streets to welcome the bride and groom. There was singing, shouting and the men shot their guns in the air in celebration. Eventually most of the people entered the church for the wedding ceremony. Many could not get in as the crowd was too big, so they stood outside of the church and waited for the bride and groom to come out. As the newly married couple emerged from the church the crowd shouted and sang and danced in celebration of the marriage. The crowd returned to Tom's mother's home and the feasting began. The merrymaking of eating, singing and dancing lasted for hours and finally the young couple left for their honeymoon and gradually the crowd dispersed. Tom and Frances were exhausted and went to bed but Tom, in spite of his fatigue was pleased that he had been able to be present and to help his young brother Elias with this most important day of his life.

On November 16, 1947 it was time for Tom, Frances and Juanita to leave Ain Arab, All of the pain that Tom had felt when he had left his homeland thirty-seven years before returned. He and his mother held each other for many minutes, each one unable to speak and Tom knew in his heart, that he would never see his mother alive again. They quickly boarded the bus to take them to Beirut and Tom was grateful that his brothers were there to console his mother after he left. No one spoke as they rode to Beirut and Tom was lost in thought. After staying overnight in Beirut they boarded the ship that would return them to America. The trip back to the states was uneventful, long and tiring and when they arrived in New York on December 2, 1947 they were glad to be back in America and Tom was at peace with himself that he had seen his mother once more. They returned to Los Angeles via Cedar Rapids and on arriving home were greeted by their beloved family.

Tom and Frances Haddy

XXV

Life took on a peaceful pattern for Tom. As the years went by his children became established in their own careers and in their own families. In 1948 John sold his share of the market that he co-owned with Joe and George to them and returned to Albert Lea, Minnesota to open an egg business.

On May 24, 1948 Vernita and Gene became the proud parents of a boy whom they named Donald Samuel. He was born in Cedar Rapids, Iowa. On February 22, 1950 Vernita and Gene gave him a granddaughter whom they named Karen Sue. She was born in Cedar Rapids, Iowa, and on October 20, 1950 Beatrice and Wadiea became parents of his grandson, Wayne John Abraham who was born in Joice, Iowa. In the year 1950 Tom sold his market to George and Lucille and invested the proceeds in real estate. Joe, a reservist in the Army was recalled into the Army in 1950 because of the Korean War and sold his share of the market to George Shaheen and his sister Selma.

Tom's family suffered a major tragedy in this year of 1950. Tom and Frances were devastated when they were told that Vernita and Gene had lost their son Donald, who was two years old. He had run into the street and had been struck by a truck and had been instantly killed. The family gathered in Cedar Rapids and mourned the loss of this precious child.

On January 8, 1950 Francis and Theresa became the parents of their first child, whom they named Richard Ian. Richard was born in Rochester, Minnesota. And on January 4. 1951 Lucille and George made Tom a proud grandfather once again as their son, named Steven Michael was born in Santa Monica, California. And in this year of 1951 Tom's younger son Francis would finish his training in internal medicine at the Mayo Clinic in Minnesota.

When he reentered the Army Joe served two years training soldiers in tank destroyer warfare. At the end of those two years, in 1952, he returned to Albert Lea, Minnesota to join his brother-in-law John in his egg business.

Tom would once more have to suffer the pain of losing a parent for in 1952 he received a letter from his bothers that their mother had passed away. Tom retreated to his bedroom to suffer his pain alone. His thought when he left Ain Arab in 1947 that he would never again see his mother alive was now a reality. His memories flashed back to the early years of his childhood and the many hours that he had spent with her. He thought of all the things that she had taught him. He remembered how she and he would spend hours drying food on the flat top of their home in preparation for the winter months. He remembered all of the love and care that she had given him. He allowed the hot tears to wash over him in an attempt to ease the pain but it would be many months before the pain would subside just as it was still painful to think of his father six years after his death. It was a pain that only immigrants who had left loved ones far behind to come to America would understand.

The life cycle of life and death continued for Tom's family.

On February 13, 1953 in St. Paul, Minnesota Francis and Theresa had a daughter whom they named Carol Elaine.

Another tragedy would strike the Haddy clan when Tom received a call from Joe and Rae, who were living in Albert Lea, Minnesota, that Tom's oldest grandchild, Sharon was stricken with the deadly paralytic disease, Polio. Tom's heart ached for his small granddaughter's misfortune.

Tom and Frances decided to go to Albert Lea to visit their granddaughter who had been placed in the Kenny Institute in Minneapolis for treatment of the devastation of the polio that racked her body. She would remain in that institution for one year. As Joe, Rae, Tom and Frances were riding from Albert Lea to Minneapolis Frances began to think about Joe's recently telling them that he had chosen Lutheranism as his religious denomination. She had been bitter about his choice and saw it as another indication of his rejection of his heritage. She began to question Rae intimating that she was at fault for Joe's renouncing his orthodox faith and embracing Lutheranism. Joe was angered at his mother's treatment of his wife. He stopped the car and told his parents firmly that they would have to accept the changes in his life that he had chosen and they were not to interfere. Frances, who had great difficulty in hiding her disappointment that her sons had not married women of

Lebanese descent fell silent. Her discontent with her children choosing other than the Lebanese culture for their own families caused strains in the family relations and when they were alone Tom tried to gently tell her that if she wanted her children to remain close to the family she would have to accept their decisions where their own lives were concerned and that in America marrying others of a different cultural or ethnic background was not unusual. Frances regretted that she had spoken of her feelings and vowed that she would try not to interfere with her children's lives. But the immigrants's deeply ingrained stubborn belief that their ethnic background should remain 'pure' is difficult to erase. This is a belief rooted in the fear of losing their children and not being able to understand or fit into the cultures of their chosen spouses. But through the years Frances would continue to be devoted to her children and gradually accept their choices for spouses.

In 1954 Joe and John, Elizabeth's husband, bought a wholesale egg business in Phoenix, Arizona. Joe and Rae had decided that the warm climate of Phoenix would be better for Sharon who was now confined to a wheelchair. The deadly destruction of polio had destroyed her ability to walk and moving about in a wheelchair would be a permanent part of her life.

In 1954 Francis called from Chicago, where he was now teaching at Northwestern School of Medicine, to say that he would be recalled into the Army to finish his obligation to the government for the education that he had received when he was in medical school. He would serve for another two years: first as a Captain, then as a Major, and finally as A Lieutenant Colonel, before returning to civilian life.

In 1955 Lucille and George would sell the market that Tom had sold them and open a restaurant on Hillhurst Avenue in Los Angeles. Tom was delighted that the family enterprises were expanding. He had invested his money in real estate and was busy with the work of managing the seventeen properties that he owned and working to make the dream of a cathedral for the orthodox church a reality. Tom would play a large role in helping to raise the three-quarters of a million dollars that would be spent to complete the Saint Nicholas Orthodox Church. The church would later be designated as a Cathedral. He felt very good about the work that he did to help to build this church. He felt that in doing so he was serving the God that had been so good to him in his life. For he knew that without his faith he never would have been able to have faced the many hardships that he and Frances had faced in trying to succeed in having the general merchandise business and in raising his seven children.

XXVI

Tom and other Lebanese-Christians felt a steadfast bond between themselves and the ancient church to which they belonged. Many of his ancestors and those of his friends had died in Lebanon simply because they were Lebanese-Christians. The age old hostilities in the region of the Lebanon were rooted in the religious differences of the Orthodox and Roman Christians and the Moslems of that region. The centuries old turmoil was fueled by the many interferences of Western and neighboring Eastern powers for political control of the area.

His religious heritage stemmed from the Patriarchate of Antioch. One of the major centers of Christianity, Antioch was historically recognized as the Queen City and capital of the Roman Diocese in the East. After the fifth century, Rome, Constantinople, Antioch, Alexandria and Jerusalem were the five major centers of Christianity, the pentarchy of Sees.

This Patriarchate of Antioch traced its beginnings to, and was founded by St. Peter the Apostle in A.D. 34. It was in the city of Antioch that followers of Christ were derisively called Christians. In the early part of the fifth century, Antioch was the religious center for the Christians of Syria, Cyprus, Arabia, Mesopotamia and Palestine. But in succeeding centuries this Antiochal See declined in size as the Byzantine Empire was faced with the threat of attacks by the Persians to the East of them. Faced with the threat of invasion, the then Byzantine Emperor Heraclius attempted to unify the religious sects so that he could present a united front of his people to the Persians but the Orthodox Christians of Antioch would not accept any compromise of their beliefs to accommodate political problems of the Emperor. And although this period of time was difficult for the Christians of Antioch, as they were subjected to earthquakes, invasions, attacks and hostile occupation by religious and cultural enemies, they steadfastly maintained their faith and survived the onslaughts of outside forces. In the early sixth century Islam rose as a major threat to the Christians in the Patriarchate of Antioch. Antioch was the first city to fall to the advance of the Moslems and they soon overran Jerusalem and Alexandria. The Christians at Antioch were then ordered to speak and celebrate their liturgical services in Arabic only replacing the Greek linguistic influence of that time. This was an attempt by the occupying forces to reduce the Byzantine influences on the Christians of the area.

The interferences of outside and hostile forces continued in the Antiochian See and although in the tenth century the area was recaptured by the Byzantines the Turks recaptured the city in 1086. Although this occupation was short it was the time of the Crusades and the armies from the West began to invade and occupy the area. The turmoil continued through the years and with it the Antioch See suffered and was reduced in size and membership.

Although they had been victims of outside forces for centuries the Orthodox faithful held to their beliefs and in the 1800's with help from the Russian Empire slowly began to recover from the constant battering to which they had been subjected. In the early nineteen hundreds the Patriarchate of Antioch started a youth movement to revitalize the See and the twentieth century would see these devoted Christians rebuild their religious heritage and flourish.

Tom was indeed proud to be a part of this inspiring saga of his religious heritage. And any work that he could do to help with the establishment of an American Cathedral for his Orthodox religion in California would be a part of his legacy to his adopted land.

XXVII

On October 10, 1956 Tom became a grandfather once more as Joe and Rae became the parents of a baby girl whom they named Michelle Juanita. She was born in Phoenix, Arizona. And on January 2, 1958 Francis and Theresa became the parents of the last of his grandchildren, Alice Elizabeth, who was born in Chicago, Illinois.

Tom served on the board of directors of St. Nicholas church from 1948, when the group of dedicated Lebanese-Christians had started plans to build their Cathedral, until 1960. He had worked tirelessly on fund raisers and had attended numerous planning meetings as one of the dedicated workers who brought the dream of a Cathedral for their Orthodox church to fruition.

Now Tom began to think that he should start to find ways for his large family to remain close and not let the distances between the various members of the clan cause them to drift apart. He thought that one way that he could accomplish keeping the family close was to have regular family reunions. So he began to write to several members of the family to see if there was any interest in getting together.

Many said that they would be interested and Tom formed a committee consisting of several of his relatives in Cedar Rapids, Iowa: Eugene Haddy, his son-in-law, Sam Mike Haddy, Tom George Haddy, George Alberts and George Ferris. In addition John Haddy of Albert Lea, Minnesota, another-son-in-law and Joe, his son and he rounded out the committee membership. This committee would plan the event and take care of the endless details necessary for such an undertaking. They only had three months before the planned date of the first reunion and there was much to be done. Tom relished the thought of engineering a large and successful family reunion.

On the 16th and 17th of July, 1960, in Cedar Rapids, Iowa the Haddys celebrated as a family with a picnic and dinner. One hundred and twenty five members of the extended family attended.

On July 16th, 1960 the picnic was held at the Beaver Park Pavillion, which had been rented for the occasion. There was Lebanese dancing and games and prizes for the children. But most of all there was talking, as the many members of the Haddy extended family came together to get to know each other. It was an opportunity to strengthen family ties and to instill in the children the age old cultural heritage of the Lebanese people. Tom was elated at the friendship and love that the participants showed.

On Sunday morning July 17th, 1960 the members of the Haddy families attended church in one of the two Orthodox churches in town, St. George or St. John. And on Sunday evening there was a dinner at the Flame Room in Tom's son-in-law Eugene and daughter Vernita's restaurant.

At the reunion Tom announced a creed written by Johann Wolfgang von Goethe that expressed Tom's wishes for his extended family and one that he hoped they would adopt....

"Health enough to make work a pleasure

Wealth enough to support your needs

Strength enough to battle with difficulties and overcome them.

Grace enough to confess your sins and forsake them

Patience enough to toil until good is accomplished

Charity enough to see some good in your neighbor

Love enough to move you to be useful and helpful to others

Faith enough to make real the things of God

Hope enough to remove all anxious fears concerning the future

    J.W. vonGoethe"

The happy participants ended the first of the Haddy family reunions with a sense of excitement as they knew that this was but the first of a yearly event to which they would look forward.

XXVIII

Tom was pleased that his daughter Beatrice, her husband Wadiea and their two sons Tom and Wayne who had been living in Joice, Iowa were moving to Los Angeles in 1960 and would be living nearby. He enjoyed having family members close to him and to be able to see them frequently.

He continued to care for the rental properties that he owned and were now his source of income, to be involved in and work for the Orthodox Cathedral that he had helped bring into being and to plan the yearly family reunions to keep the various members of the clan in touch with each other.

The second reunion was also held in Cedar Rapids, Iowa. On the evening of July 14th, 1961 Tom hosted an evening in the Cedar Rapids St. Georges church basement for all to gather and greet each other on this second Haddy family reunion. There were one hundred and fifty people in attendance.

On Saturday a picnic was held. One hundred and seventy-five people gathered in the rain. The menu reflected the LebaneseAmerican culture of the participants. Kibbee, suf, ham, homas, baked beans, vegetables, Syrian bread, hard rolls, coffee, soft drinks and icecream. There was an open bar for beer or mixed-drinks. Eugene Haddy prepared the delicious food.

On Sunday July 16, 1961 there was an evening banquet at the Montrose Hotel's Crystal Ballroom that one hundred and forty people attended. There was a cocktail hour at 5:00 o'clock and at 7:00 a dinner and program. The menu consisted of swiss steak and all the trimmings prepared by the hotel. Taft Haddy of Tryon, Nebraska was the master of ceremonies. At 9:00 the dancing began with the Tom Kacere band, and the crowd exuberantly danced the Dubkee and Ruhssa.

On Sunday morning they attended one of the two Orthodox churches of Cedar Rapids, St. Georges and St. Johns. The second reunion, like the first, was a success with the clansmen parting thinking of next year's get-to-gether.

The Haddy reunions were being eagerly attended by the members of his extended family and Tom was very happy for it was evident that all of them felt as he did that close family ties were important and that the reunions gave those that attended a chance to strengthen those ties. Members of the family were forming friendships with each other that they had never experienced before and their mutual family ties gave them a foundation upon which to build those friendships. But more importantly, in Tom's view, the young people of the Haddy families were being given a sense of their Lebanese heritage. Tom thought that these reunions were accomplishing the same thing that the village gatherings that he attended in Ain Arab as a boy accomplished, where he heard the stories of the ancient history of The Lebanon. The heritage and its meaning was being passed on to the younger generation. But that heritage had expanded to include the cultures into which the immigrant Lebanese had moved and which was a large part of their sons and daughters and their children's lives.

The third Haddy reunion was held in Los Angeles, California on the 15th, 16th, and 17th of June of 1962. So many were coming to the event from the mid-west that Tom decided that they should reserve a railroad coach so that they could travel together. He contacted the office of the Southern Pacific railroad. They were happy to accommodate him and sent information on schedules and costs which he sent to the various members of the family in the mid-west so that they could plan their travel schedules. Tom thought that the trip out to the west coast would be several extra hours that the members of the clan could visit and enjoy one another. He thought that anyway that he could build friendship and comradeship amongst the family members would strengthen the ties and that was his intent.

On Friday evening of the weekend Nemer T. Nemer, Frances' brother-in-law prepared a dinner for the eighty people who attended and it was served in the church parlors of St. Mary's Episcopal Church. The group then socialized and caught up on events that had occurred since the last reunion. One of the group, Toofik Simon and his sons provided Lebanese music for dancing.

On Saturday, the 16th one hundred and five Haddy Family members went to Griffith Park in Los Angeles for a picnic lunch which was prepared by Lucille's husband, George. There was more Lebanese music and many of the group played ball games.

On Sunday morning all of the group attended church at St. Nicholas Cathedral. The children in attendance were learning that the faith of their people was a major part of their lives.

On Sunday evening there was a cocktail hour at the Knickerbocker Hotel in California and Tom's cousin Mike Haddy's son-in-law, Kew Slaughter, acted as bartender. He prepared strawberry pop 'cocktails' for the children who were excited at being included in their parents activities.

Ninety people attended and a dance band provided music for the teenagers to dance and a huge cake, donated by Juanita Haddy, to celebrate Father's Day was enjoyed by the crowd. Tom announced that there were 125 Haddy families throughout the world and every one clapped furiously. The familial bonds were being strengthened. It was a fun-filled evening for all who were there. Sadly, it would be the last family gathering in the life of Nemer T. Nemer for shortly after the reunion he passed away. Tom was deeply saddened by Nemer's death for he and Frances' sister Selma, Nemer's wife, had been close family members of Tom's for years. They had worked and shared his life and he had shared theirs. As the clan grew in number with the marriage of the young members and the children born to them Tom was pleased, but, as they began to lose some of his generation of members he was saddened. The life cycle went on.

Tom felt a warm glow of happiness as his thoughts turned to the large family of which he was the 'Patriarch'. He thought of the many members of his extended family that attended the yearly family reunions. And he felt a sense of pride, for this large group of immigrants, their children and their children's children were now Americans. They had built businesses, large and small. They had built homes and a church where they worshiped in freedom without worrying about invasions from foreign lands. Many had served, with honor, in the armed services of this country to which their parents had emigrated. Many of them were doctors, lawyers, politicians, and businessmen and women. Yes, Tom was proud and pleased when he thought of his extended family and the reunions were providing the new generations of Haddys with a sense of pride in their Lebanese heritage. And he reflected on the meaning of the ancestral family name, El Hadi, ...quiet and content.

The year of 1963 passed quietly as Tom and other members of the Haddy Families planned the next reunion which would be held in Phoenix, Arizona during the month of February in 1964.

On February 8th, 1964 Frances complained of chest pains and was hospitalized. Dr. Nicola sadly told Tom that she had suffered a heart attack. Tom found a quiet corner in the hospital chapel and prayed for his beloved wife's health. Frances had had times when she did not feel well over the years but there had never been a time when her health problems had been serious. It was twelve days before Tom and Frances' fiftieth wedding anniversary and a dinner celebrating that event had been planned. A large 50th wedding anniversary dinner had been planned at the Roosevelt Hotel in Los Angeles. The many guests that had been invited were contacted and told that the dinner would be canceled. Now Tom's concern for his wife's health overshadowed any of his thoughts about reunions and dinners.

She returned home two weeks after her hospital admission and Tom was relieved that she had recovered from the attack enough to be allowed to return home. Frances was happy to be home and told Tom that she wanted him to go to the family reunion in spite of the fact that she could not attend. Tom argued that he would not attend but Frances was insistent that he go.

So in response to her wishes Tom attended the fourth reunion which was held in Phoenix, Arizona on February 28th and 29th of 1964. On Friday evening, February 28th cocktails and dinner were served in the recreation hall of Phoenix's St. George's Orthodox Church for all members of the families and their close friends. After a short business meeting of the officers of the Haddy Clan committee, John Haddy, who was serving as President for that year introduced Joe Haddy who served as master of ceremonies for the reunion. He announced that there would be an open house on Sunday from 2:00 p.m. to 5:00 p.m. at the home of George Shaheen. The open house would be hosted by Mr. and Mrs. Joseph G. Haddy, Mr. and Mrs. Albert M. Haddy and Mr. and Mrs. George J. Shaheen.

On Saturday, February 29th groups of those attending played golf or went bowling and groups of the women shopped and visited to gossip. On Saturday evening at 5:00 o'clock cocktails were served at the Sands Hotel in Phoenix and the cocktail hour was followed by a dinner. One hundred and fifty seven people attended.

For the first time Tom was attending a reunion alone. He felt saddened and could not bring himself to enjoy what had become to him, an important part of his life. The observance of his and Frances' 50th golden wedding anniversary had been a quiet time by his wife's bedside before he had left for the reunion. His mind kept wandering back to Frances and her health and he silently prayed to his God that she would improve.

Sixty people attended the open house that was held on Sunday after most of those attending the reunion had attended the churches in Phoenix. It was announced that there are 450 members of Haddy Families that can trace their ancestry back to George El Haddy who lived one-hundred and fifty years earlier.

The fourth Haddy family reunion was a success like the ones before it but the shadow of Frances' grave illness overshadowed the celebration of the reunion for Tom and his sons and daughters. Through the Spring and Summer of 1964 Tom stayed close to home and watched over Frances who had recovered from her heart attack but was much weaker than before. She was much less able to do the many things that had been so much of her life. Her daughters, Lucille, Juanita and Beatrice and her sister Selma who lived nearby spent a great deal of time with her as she tried to regain her health and she was grateful for their and Tom's presence. But her progress back to good health was slow.

On a warm September day in this year of 1964 Tom sat in his favorite chair and read an essay that his grandson and namesake, Tom Abraham, had written as an English assignment in school. Tom was eleven years old. Tom was very proud of his grandchildren and the fact that they wrote stories about him as school assignments pleased him.
The essay read....

> *"The Man Who Did The Impossible*
> *Tom Haddy overcame hardship by his will. He was born in the 1890's in Lebanon. Tom grew up as a shepherd boy. When in the field, he, with his dog, would lay for hours dreaming of the land of opportunity." The United States of America." "Someday I am going to live in the United States", he would say hopefully to his dog. Tom's mother and father were always good to him, and today, Tom believes, that without them, he would still be in Lebanon herding sheep.*
>
> *Their dream was to have him live in America. After much toiling and saving, Tom's parents finally had enough money to send their son to America.*
>
> *At the age of eighteen, alone and without knowing the English language, Tom boarded a ship heading for the United*

States. He still remembers the great thrill of seeing America for the first time. The dream, of his parents and his own had finally come true.

After leaving the ship, his destination was Iowa, where his Uncle was living. Not having enough money, he knew he had to earn his way. He started working in his uncles' grocery store. He was slowly learning the English language. Finally, he had saved enough money and was on his way to Minnesota. Tom fell in love with Minnesota, and soon had settled down in Walters. He could speak the English language fluently now. He married a woman who had also come from Lebanon. He started up a grocery store and started another one at Kiester, Minnesota.

Tom and his wife had seven beautiful children. He vowed that he could bring his family up just like his father had done, and Tom did just that. I will never forget the time he told me that he was the first person in town to have an indoor bathroom.

After Tom's family grew up, he and his wife moved to Los Angeles. He is retired now, but he doesn't have anything to be sad about. His happiness is in his children. Five of the girls are all housewives. One of his boys is President of a large produce plant in Phoenix, Arizona. The other one is Chairman of the Physiology Department at the University of Oklahoma.

I should be proud also, because Tom Haddy, the person whom I was named after, is my Grandfather.

Tom Abraham"

As he laid the letter aside, Tom reflected on the joy that his large family brought to him. His beautiful grandchildren would carry on the legacy of honor that his grandfather and those before him gave to his father; that his father, in turn, had given to him; and that he, in turn, had given to his children, who would pass the legacy on to their children and they to their children.

XXIX

In the Summer of 1965 Frances had regained some of her strength but Tom still worried about her. He had been thinking that he would like to visit his brothers and their families back in Ain Arab but he was reluctant to go. Frances knew that his family was on his mind and insisted that he go alone. She would stay with their daughter Vernita, who lived in Iowa, while he was gone. He finally agreed to the arrangement and on June 12 made a return trip to his village to see his relatives. While she stayed with Vernita and her family, Frances was visited by her other children, who also lived in the midwest. Elizabeth and John were in Albert Lea, Minnesota and Francis and Theresa were in Oklahoma City, Oklahoma, where Francis was Chairman of the Department of Physiology at the University of Oklahoma, School of Medicine.

Upon his return from Ain Arab, Tom spent more and more time with Frances as her illness had upset him badly. Although she had recovered to the point where she could visit with friends and do light chores it was obvious to Tom that she had lost a great deal of her vigor. The Fall months passed quietly and Tom's fears of Frances' poor health were not unfounded.

On December 24, 1965 Frances suffered her second heart attack and was again hospitalized. She became bedridden and although she was allowed to return home after being treated for the second heart attack she would have to return to the hospital repeatedly as her health deteriorated. Tom spent all of his time with her now and devoted himself to caring for her. He was heartbroken that this vibrant woman that he so dearly loved was so weak and ill.

In the early morning hours of April 6, 1966 Frances awakened Tom to tell him that she was not feeling well and Tom asked Juanita, who lived with them, to call the doctor. At 5:00 a.m. as he and Juanita sat talking to Frances while they waited for the doctor, she closed her eyes and passed away.

Juanita rushed to call the emergency service. Tom looked at his wife and was gripped with fear. He went to her side and shook her violently praying that she would respond. She did not. Slowly, his mind told him that she was gone. He gathered her into his arms as he was engulfed in fear and panic. In an emotional turmoil he cried out for his beloved wife to come back. The hot tears streamed down his face and the pain of his loss washed over him. The paramedics arrived and attempted to revive her but they knew that revival techniques were useless. Tom watched as they worked on her and prepared to take her to the hospital. He was numb with grief. His Frances had died. It was not possible!

Beatrice and Lucille were called and came to Tom's side. The others; Joseph, Francis, Vernita and Elizabeth, were notified of the loss of their mother. The devastation that they felt was indescribable. Frances had devoted her life to her children and her husband. They were her life and now she was gone. Acceptance of that fact would come slowly to all of them.

They began to notify other relatives and friends of Frances' death and to make the necessary funeral arrangements. Calls and telegrams began to pour in as Frances had touched many lives besides those of her husband and children.

On Sunday evening, April 10, 1966 a prayer service was held for Frances in the Cathedral of St. Nicholas in Los Angeles. And on Monday April 11, 1966 she was laid to rest at Forest Lawn Memorial Park. Tom sat holding the memorial card dedicated to his wife as he read the scripture that they had picked for her.....

"The Lord is my shepherd; I shall not want.
He maketh me to lie down in green pastures; he leadeth
me beside the still waters.
He restoreth my soul; he leadeth me in the path of
righteousness for his name's sake.
Yea, though I walk through the valley of the shadow
of death, I will fear no evil; for thou art with me;
thy rod and thy staff they comfort me.
Thou preparest a table before me in the presence of mine
enemies: Thou anointest my head with oil; my cup runneth
over.

*Surely goodness and mercy shall follow me all the days
of my life; and I will dwell in the house of the Lord
forever.*

> *.....the twenty-third psalm"*

The age old words comforted him and eased some of his pain.

For I have given you an example.

Icon painted in memory of Frances. Donated by Tom and their children

St Nicholas Church that Tom helped to build.

XXX

The weeks following Frances' death moved slowly for Tom. A numbness came over him and the emptiness left by her departure permeated his home. He was melancholy and had little interest in eating or sleeping. He spent much of his time in his room as his mind was flooded with the many memories of his life with her. They had been married for fifty-three years and life without her seemed impossible to him. His children tried to console him but he had retreated into his memories and did not respond to their efforts.

As the weeks slipped by he began to think of how he could provide a memorial to Frances' life and thought that a mural on the wall of the Cathedral would last for centuries and keep Frances' memory alive. His mind focused on this memorial and he dedicated himself to making it a reality. He contacted his children and told them of his plans. He requested that they participate and that he and each of them would share the cost so that it would be a family gift to Frances. He contacted his friend and religious father, Father Paul Romley of the Cathedral. Father Romley presented Tom's request to the Church board and they agreed to allow the mural in Frances' memory to be painted. The theme of the mural would be taken from the biblical text of St. John 13: 1-17; the historic moment in the life of Christ, where he turned to his disciples after the Last Supper and washed their feet. An example of the humility that was a part of his teachings.

The mural would be situated on the south-east wall of the Cathedral and would be twenty-five feet in height and eleven feet wide. Mr. Inocenzio Dario of Beverly Hills, California was chosen as the artist. The mural would be done on a canvas with rich oil paints and Mr. Dario told Tom that he would use a neo-Byzantine style in the painting of the mural. Each of the disciples and Christ would be painted as if they were individual portraits.

The work on the mural began and Tom would visit the church each day to watch the artist work. The project became the center of his life as it was being developed and he immersed himself in it as it was his link to Frances. He was sure that she too was watching and was pleased with this memorial that he had planned. It would last for centuries and her memory with it. The mural took months to finish and in November of 1966 it was completed and dedicated to Frances. Tom's heart was heavy with despair and he returned home where he went to his room to be alone with his heartache. He picked up a pen and began to write what was in his heart. He wrote.....

"WHERE'S THE REST OF ME..?

The most important thing a man can know is that, as he approaches his own door, someone on the other side is listening for the sound of his footsteps. Yes, where is the one, that her and I were to celebrate our 50th Golden Wedding Anniversary, together with our family, relatives and friends, in the Roosevelt Hotel in Hollywood, California on February 22, 1964.

Over four hundred invitations were mailed out, over four hundred friends responded and were glad to help us celebrate that event, many presents arrived at our home and they will be kept for the memory of that day; that day that never came true. Instead, on February 8th at 10:00 o'clock p.m. 1964, my beloved wife Frances was struck with a heart attack. Of course, Dr. George Nicola, lost no time in sending her to Hollywood Presbyterian Hospital in care of Dr. Mc Nabb, a heart specialist. With all the good care that she received, in thirty days she came home believing that her heart had healed. Through the summertime, going weekly to her doctor for her check up, until that winter when she came down with diarrhea, which her doctor could not completely cure. On May 18, 1965, we went to the Mayo Brothers Clinic in Rochester, Minnesota. After ten days examination, they found nothing seriously wrong, so they prescribed a pill for her, which gave her relief from the diarrhea.

Her weight went down from 155 pounds to 115 pounds but soon after she began to gain weight, by eating normal food. On June 12, 1965 I left her with our daughter Vernita in Cedar Rapids, Iowa and went to Lebanon to visit my three brothers and their families. It was her decision that I must go while she was visiting with our children in the middle west, Elizabeth and John in Albert Lea, Minn. Gene and Vernita in Cedar Rapids, Iowa and our son Dr. Francis Haddy and his wife in Oklahoma City, Oklahoma. On August 21, 1965 I was back home and she also was back home, looking and feeling fine, her weight was 135 lbs.

On October 1, 1965 I was taken to the hospital for a cold and pneumonia, after ten days of good care I came home and recovered fine, then on Good Friday evening, March 1966, Frances took sick again with a heart attack, from then on most of the time she was in the hospital, until March 15, when she came home feeling much better. Dr. Mc Nabb and our son Francis together agreed to have Dr. George Groft, the top heart specialist in the western states examine her. After doing so, he prescribed different medicine for her, which relieved her of her chest pains and left her feeling good enough to come home, however, she was only home for three weeks. Then on the morning of April 6, 1966, at 5:00 o'clock in the a.m. she passed away sitting up in bed talking to me and our daughter Juanita, before the doctor could come to see her. I hope and pray no one will witness such a departing.

For two and one half years, she lived with a fear about herself, for two and a half years I lived with her, gladly waiting on her, praying to God to spare her for me and for her children. For two and one half years I asked God, please take me first for I knew that she can keep busy at her home and with our children, but God didn't want it that way, he did his will and now I am alone, lonesome days and nights, lonesome Tom without his beloved, home that was always full of his family and friends, home that always was managed perfectly, by a perfect mother and wife. Home that raised wonderful children with hard going days with her by my side, she never gave up or complained, home that began with nothing in 1914, home that was managed by a proud mother. That mother is not at home any more, to listen to the sounds of her husband's footsteps. The mother that was always proud of her husband and family and loved every one of her friends. She was proud of her work and proud of her relatives, yes, she was a proud mother. She loved every one of our relatives, she loved her friends, she loved to work, she loved to help whenever she could, she loved to do charity according to her ability, she loved her Church, she loved the Ladies Society of St. Nicholas Cathedral and loved her religion.

I know that she is happy for the painting her family donated to St. Nicholas Cathedral in her memory. It is a mural of Our Lord Jesus Christ washing the twelve apostles feet after the Last Supper, it will be seen there for centuries to come, her memory will never be forgotten.

For me her memory will be in my heart until we meet again in a better world, I know she will pray for me and help me to be with her for ever and ever, Amen.

In 1947, her, Juanita and myself went to Lebanon, to see my mother and my brothers families, my father passed away in 1946. She wrote daily happenings to us on that trip, from the day we left Los Angeles to the day we came home. Please read that! She was the one who always sent clothes and divided them among my brothers families, she never refused to help them, whether it was money or clothing.

Ever since we got married, there never was a time when she complained or refused to help my family. She was loved by every one of them. For her memory, you will see the painting of the Last Supper in St. Thomas Church in Ain Arab, Lebanon, which was donated by the family.

I don't think I can find a word good enough to describe the one I loved, of the fifty three years that she and I, working together through good times and hard times, through sickness and worry, through dark and stormy days, through sunshine and warm days.

This is the only way, I will describe her, yes, where is the rest of me?

Lonely Tom"

XXXI

In 1967 another Haddy reunion was held in Cedar Rapids, Iowa and although Tom attended he was a changed man. The joy that he had felt in attending these reunions was overshadowed by the loss of Frances. She had been as strong an advocate of keeping the family together as he had and he thought that he should do his share to keep the gatherings going but without her at his side he found it difficult to be as enthusiastic as he once had been.

He addressed the crowd as he always did and told them that the first Haddy male born in the United States was Michael Skaff of Albert Lea, Minnesota whose mother had been Dihne Haddy Skaff. And he quoted President John Kennedy who had once said, when asked about his family's solidarity, "We have been taught that families stick together through thick and thin. This will encourage respect and love and cooperation which is a very important principle of life. Without them, any family could become divided and dwindle very fast."

Tom then told the crowd, " we too must keep our family together to create unity and love. No matter how much wealth and possessions you have you will have failed in life if you do not build a strong family. Our legacy for the children must be that if you have faith in your self and believe in your self your dreams will come true. We must provide wisdom from generation to generation. Love for family and faith in yourself are the cornerstones to success. A man who dreams about the wealth of another man and wishes that he had that man's wealth wastes his time and effort in the dreaming and does not spend the time working to fulfill his dreams. Watching, wishing and even prayers will get us nowhere if we don't do something about it."

The reunion was enjoyed by the group but they all felt the loss of Frances.

The days and months slipped past and Tom busied himself with his church and his family as he had before but the loneliness did not lessen. He was in his mid-seventies now and although his health was good he found himself being less eager to be as active as he had been.

A year later he received a letter from his grandson, Wayne Abraham, and smiled to himself as he read the young man's words.

"Dear Grandpa,

Today I am eighteen years old. Legally, I am now a man. You have played a major role in my past eighteen years and you will continue to be a guiding force for me. You have made me proud of my ancestry and I am proud to be an Abraham.

Though our ages are many years apart, we are both at trying times in our life. Since Grandma died, you have had to learn how to live all over again. You have had to learn how to make the best of it until you reunite with her in the heavenly kingdom. But Grandpa never wish for death. You have too much going for you in your life.

The next four years of my life will decide my occupation in life. I just hope I can become half as successful as you are. I hope I can make you proud of me as I am of you.

Thank you very much for the birthday money. Tell everyone Hello!

Love, Wayne"

Tears came to his eyes as he read Wayne's words but there was a comfort in those tears for he still was a very proud grandfather.

XXXII

The next three years were years where Tom slowly healed from his grief. The feeling of loss would never completely leave him but he was alive and had to go on. He busied himself with writing letters to his friends and children who did not live in the immediate vicinity and devoted himself to his church and its charitable works. He made donations to the charities that were of concern to his parish and paid for many of the small needs of his church. The loneliness never left him although Juanita and a young niece of Tom's who was visiting from Lebanon were living with him.

One day Juanita came to Tom and told him that she was going to get married to one Richard Landon. Tom was happy for her as she had been with him for many years and he worried that she would be alone if he were to die. Richard and Juanita were married and Tom welcomed the last son-in-law to the family. It gave him a sense of contentment that Juanita was married and wished that Frances could have lived long enough to see the last of her daughters married.

Several months later Tom was visiting Juanita and her new husband and met a very pleasant woman named Alexandria Dibs. she too was alone and Tom soon found himself inviting her to have lunch or dinner with him. She belonged to the St. Luke' s Orthodox congregation in Garden Grove and this gave them an opportunity to be involved in the activities of both of the churches to which they belonged. Tom was grateful for the companionship that she gave him and after several months of spending time together, Tom asked Alexandria to marry him. They were quietly married in 1969. His children were surprised at his decision to remarry but understood his loneliness and were happy for his having found a companion for his latter years.

In 1971 Tom received the following letter from the President of the Board of Directors of St. Nicholas Cathedral. It read...

"My Dear brothers and sisters in Christ:
This letter is written to inform you that 1, as president of the
Board of Directors, have appointed the following parishioners
to be "honorary life member" of our Board. Because of their
years of service and their dedication and love and sacrifice for
this community, they have earned for themselves far more than
we can ever hope to give them to show our appreciation. The
worthy men appointed are:

Mr. Amean Haddad
Mr. Tom Haddy
Mr. Oscar Mitty
Mr. Salem Saba

Father Paul and I will present these brethren with special
medallions and certificates following the Divine Liturgy this
Sunday, January 19th, We know you will want to share this
program with us and personally extend your best wishes to
them.
Trusting to see you this Sunday and wishing you all a Merry
Christmas and Happy New Year, I remain,
December 14, 1971
In Christ,
Joe Wain,
President. "

This honor as life member of the Board of Directors of the St.
Nicholas Cathedral is given as in keeping with Article 4, Section 5 of the
Cathedral constitution which states, "An honorary life membership shall
be bestowed by the president upon anyone who has served on the Saint
Nicholas board of directors ten years or more." Tom, who had been one
of the founding fathers of the cathedral and had served the church faithfully
since it had been built was a worthy choice for this honor that was being
given to him.

XXXIII

Tom received a letter from his son Francis and with the letter Francis had sent him a picture of ducks. The picture brought back memories to Tom of the many gaggles of ducks that he had seen flying over Southern Minnesota in the wonderful years that he had lived there. He had received the small town newspaper, The Kiester Courier, from Kiester, Minnesota during the years since he had left that small mid-western town to move to California. He had enjoyed keeping up with the town's news as the years that he had spent in that town raising his children had been and would always be some of the best years of his life. This morning he had received a copy of the paper and Francis' picture so after reading Francis' letter and the paper he decided that he would write to the paper.
And so he wrote.....

"To the Editor:
Today I was sitting at my desk thinking about my nearly 84 years of age. Mainly, I thought about the community that I spent my younger days with, Our beginnings as a family were first in Walters, then Conger, and finally in Kiester, Minnesota. In those wonderful three small towns, we enjoyed our young life surrounded by people who were great and prosperous farmers. We gladly served them in our general merchandise store to the very best of our ability.

Between the years of 1916 through 1943, regardless of the two depressions and two wars we went through at that time, we watched the community grow. Also we watched our family and children grow-up, go to school, and enjoy their activities among all of their friend-students. We will never forget the beautiful band Kiester had in those days. They wore handsome uniforms, presented by the Late B.A. Talle-God rest his soul. Led by

Principal Olsen and band-leader Pat Phillippi the band was a prize-winner at the State Fair. The education our children received in Kiester high school has served them well and we gratefully thank the school for that.

We receive the Kiester Courier regularly since we have left the community and are able to keep abreast of the news. For that we thank that wonderful couple, Elton and Lois Matson, for putting out such a good paper and keeping those far away in touch. It means a lot.

It hurts me when I read that some of the old-timers we used to serve have passed away. We always respected them and they must have respected us to let us participate in their community affairs. For instance, after we incorporated the town of Walters, a few years later, 1, myself, was elected mayor of the town. During my term we brought the electric light from Albert Lea to Walters without a penny cost to the town. Blue Earth attorneys, Grundy and Morris, were our attorneys. Then I served as treasurer for the Woodman lodge. The late Otto Koetke and myself organized the Merchants Egg Association in Walters. I helped to open the State Bank of Walters. Unfortunately in a few years the bank closed their doors but there were no losses to any of the shareholders.

On the recreational side I was the pitcher for the soft-ball team in Walters and I must say we did a pretty good job.

In Kiester, when the late B.A. Talle was there, I was one of the five persons signing notes to the bank for the purpose of building the Kiester Theater. So you see, how can we forget those days living among such wonderful communities like Walters, Conger and Kiester. The second world war took our boys, my son-in-law John Haddy in the Walters store, my brother-in-law, George Shaheen in the Conger store and our two boys, Joe and Francis. Their absence and the fact that my late wife became ill caused us to move to a warmer climate or I can assure you, I would have been with you today.

Here in Hollywood, California, since 1943 I have been associated with the community leaders of our Eastern Orthodox Church. With many others in our community we built a cathedral and a hall that cost over three million dollars. I have been a member of the Board of Directors since 1948 and I will die an honorary member. This made our family very happy and content, thank God. However, please believe me, no matter how old I am or how far I have moved away, I will be thinking of you the rest of my days. God bless you all, old and young.

    I wrote these words to tell you it was an honor to raise my wonderful family among your great community, Thank you and God bless you all. I used to put out this slogan on your general calls to the farmers of the community. Please remember- I am still "At your service

Sincerely,
T.J. Haddy
4407 Prospect, Apt. 5
Los Angeles, CA 90027"

    By writing to the Kiester Courier and in reaching out to one of the small mid-western towns where he had made his living and raised his family in the early years of his marriage Tom would stir the memories of his old neighbors and friends. Although over thirty years had passed since he had left that small town several took the time to respond. He felt a warm glow as he read their replies. One in particular touched his heart. It read....

"30 October 1975

Dear Mr. Haddy,

    I don't know if you remember me or not but I'm sure you remember my father and mother Arnold and Marie Steinhauer, my grandparents the G.H. Steinhauers and the George Ensers.

    What has prompted me to write this letter is your letter in the Kiester Courier, this week. It is wonderful to read your letter and share the nice feelings about the communities we both have.

    As you know Tom, I grew up in the Walters community and well I remember the "Haddy Store", how I looked forward to the free show nights and the Saturday nights for shopping. And well I remember you Tom, you always had a word for us kids and that meant a lot. It even means more now as I look back, that you always had the time to say hello and ask how I was. I'm sure those communities of Conger, Walters and Kiester, were what they were because of people like you, and that I am what I am because of the good influence and example you set. I'm sure most of the people of those communities appreciate them, but as you well know if one moves away I think it really makes you more appreciative. My dad and mother and Hilbert, still live on the farm and are enjoying their retirement. They have their health and manage very well.

I don't know when the last time was that you were in Walters, but it isn't like we like to remember it any more. They say it is progress that does away with the little towns-if that is progress we can do without it, so far as I'm concerned. I'm sure if their were more communities like that today we would not have the young people problems we do. Those communities were because of people like you Tom Haddy, and I'm happy that your life influenced mine in the town of Walters, and I'm sure I am better because of it. You are nearly 84 and I am 46 and I have three children 21, 18 and 13. I wish they could have known the Haddy Store and the friendly times, laughter and all the other good things it brought me. I've told my wife and them about it often.

The best to you Tom, and I'll say Hello from my folks too as I'm sure if they knew I was writing to you they would tell me to. Thanks for writing that letter in the Kiester paper-I'm sure I'm not the only one that appreciated it.

> *Very respectfully,*
> *Bernard C. Steinhauer"*

Tom had shared this beautiful letter with his pastor, Father Paul Romley of the Cathedral and he was touched by Father Romley's response to Bernard Steinhauer. It read....

"Dear Mr. Steinhauer:

I was visiting with one of the founders of our Cathedral today. Mr. Tom Haddy, and during that visit he showed me a copy of your newspaper in which he wrote an article. He received your response, and I had the good fortune of reading your letter with him.

I couldn't let another minute go by without answering you. Your letter was beautiful- very beautiful. It's so refreshing to hear about and read about people like you. To write the way you did to "Uncle Tom", you and your people certainly must be wonderful. I'm thinking of using your beautiful letter in one of my sermons. May Cod bless you and your family always. You are right about

Uncle Tom- he is a very precious man and certainly, as you put it, our life is better for having been blessed with his presence.
                              In Christ
                              Father Paul"

Another response read.....

"Dear Mr. Haddy,
(or Tom, as I prefer to remember you)
       You probably do not remember me, but I enjoyed seeing your letter in the "Courier" and also the one you wrote at the time of the Diamond Jubilee, and I felt I must write to you.
       I have so many wonderful memories of going to Walters with my folks, Alvina and Albert Yonkey and shopping at Haddys and Koetkes and then later shopping at Haddys in Kiester. My dad, being crippled couldn't do many things, but he could drive the team on our old surrey.
       I was so thrilled to have Francis at our pageant at Kiester together with John and Elizabeth. Carl and I are still on our farm that was originally my father's and my grandfather's homestead and we really enjoy being a part of the community you spoke of in your letters.
       Both of our children live within 80 rods of us -Don on the old Leschefski farm which he bought, and Karlene, in a home on the corner south of us from where her husband conducts a very successful electrical service.
       Our three grandchildren go to the Kiester school and help Carl and me keep in touch with the younger generation which is wonderful for us. Our oldest grandson's picture (Danny Gormley) is in the Courier this week showing his safety poster.
       Thank you, Tom, for sharing your memories with us. You've helped make this a wonderful world.
                       All our love-Ruby and Carl Nore
                       May God continue to bless you and yours
                              (Ruby Yonkey)"

And still another read....

> *"Dearfriend TJ. Haddy,*
>
> *When George and I read your letter in the Kiester paper of October 19th we both said we would have to answer it right away. Here it is two months later. Now its Christmas season, what can be a better gift than take the time and reminisce. We both remember when you first arrived in our community, I as Frieda Behr, daughter of Fred Behr of Conger and married George Neve of Walters.*
>
> *The store in Conger was a busy place and guess we certainly can say that of Walters too. We loved all you Haddy families, got to know you so well here in Walters.*
>
> *Still see John and Elizabeth occasionally in the mall in Albert Lea, and they never forget a funeral of old friends.*
>
> *We have a family of three girls, married. Phyllis married to Lloyd Meyer, living on the old Barney Meyer farm. Eunice married, living in Mankato, Glennyce the youngest one went to Tanzania, Africa for two years teaching, came home and married a minister and they live in Nebraska.*
>
> *Have two grandchildren married. Steve interested in ministry and have three granddaughters in nursing.*
>
> *Now our family consists of 27 people. We'll have most of them here for Christmas. George was 77 years young in Oct. working every day, says he enjoys it. We're both in the best of health. Do you remember when we stopped at your house several years ago and you found a motel for us, it was a big beautiful place on the outside but oh so dirty on the inside, it was in the evening, we had stayed a little too late at your house and were only too glad to get the kids to bed. It made us get up earlier in the morning and we were on our way again. I worked as cook in our Walters school here for 22 years and enjoyed it very much, and retired at 68 years young. As you're getting the Kiester Courier you see we've lost our lovely school here of which we feel bad, tried hard to keep it. George built the school, I spent 28 years, our three girls and 14 of our grandchildren received their education, it really meant a lot to our family.*

*I'm sure you also read about our pot-belly stove being
stolen and is back in the jail again. A good joke.*
*Well Tom we could rattle on for a long time and not think
of all the things good and bad we might remember. So a blessed
Christmas and Happy New Year*

George and Frieda Neve
Walters, Minn"

Tom treasured these letters that revived the sweet memories of those
early years in southern Minnesota and where the future that he had dreamed
of as a shepherd boy in Ain Arab had become a reality. As an immigrant
to the United States, there could have been no better place for him to go
than the heartland of America. For it is there that a large part of the spirit
of America and the shaping of her people's character took place. And as
new Americans, Tom and his family had been shaped by the people and
the land of that mid-western region.

XXXIV

As the years slipped by The Cathedral became a place where Tom could go and feel joy and pride. He was happy to see it grow and its beauty was a source of pleasure for him. While sitting in church listening to the sermon one Sunday Tom had difficulty hearing parts of it. He was eighty-six now and his hearing was not as good as it once had been. But, discarding the thought that his diminished hearing was at fault, he decided that the problem was in the loud speaker that was being used to make the ritual and sermon heard by the congregation. He spoke with other members and they agreed that they too were having difficulty hearing the sermon. So he visited with his friend Father Romley to discuss the problem. He asked Father Romley if he could spearhead a drive to raise money to put an advanced sound system in the church and he would donate one-thousand dollars to get the fund drive started; he would eventually donate much more to the project. Father Romley smiled at his old friend and agreed that this was a good idea.

After the sound system was in operation Tom still could not hear the sermon to his satisfaction and he reluctantly admitted to himself that the problem was his own fading hearing but he had another idea. He asked the church fathers if they would consider installing earphone outlets in some of the pews for the hearing impaired. The church obliged and Tom was happy that he could sit in the pew next to the mural of his beloved wife Frances and enjoy the spiritual messages that fed his soul.

In September of 1978 Tom was given an honorary life membership to the parish council. The clergy and lay leaders of the Cathedral were very grateful for the many years of service and the many generous donations that Tom had given to the church. He truly was a pillar of the church.

Also, in the year of 1978 Tom was told by his son Joe that he and Rae were being divorced. The news saddened Tom but he did not intrude on his son's difficult decision.

On March 11, 1979 there was an installation of twenty-one new members into the Order of St. Ignatius of Antioch at Saint Nicholas. Tom was one of the newly designated Knights of Saint Ignatius. The purpose of the order was to have its members work to enhance the spiritual and humanitarian goals of the archdiocese. He then attended the prayer breakfast which was held in honor of the new members after the church service. In the evening an orthodox vesper service was held with all of the orthodox clergy of southern California in attendance. Tom was deeply moved by the solemn orthodox rituals of his installation into the Order of St. Ignatius. The many honors that the church had bestowed on him over the years gave Tom a sense of pride for he felt that in working for the church he had fulfilled another of the expectations that his father had for him, he was living his life with honor.

Although Tom's health continued to be poor, he was a lucky man for his children remained devoted to him over the years and he truly was the 'Patriarch' of the large extended family.

In March of 1980 Joe married one Doris LaVon Baker and Tom was happy for his son's new found happiness.

On July 10th 1982 they all gathered at Michaels Restaurant in Los Angeles to honor him on his 90th birthday.
He prepared a speech to give to his clan and proudly stood to deliver it. He said....

"Ladies and Gentlemen...

I have no speech-what I do have is a heart to heart talk to all of you. My wife, Alex and myself want to thank every one of you, the Haddy, Abraham, and Landon families, for your kind thoughts to have this affair for the 90th birthday for your father.

And to you dearest relatives, and friends, many thanks to you for coming to make this occasion complete. My birthday and that of my dearest Brian Abraham (a great grandson) fell on the 15th of July, so I am short of the time by 5 days. My dear daughter Beatrice and her sister Lucille made this change for a good reason. I want to thank them.

This event makes history for our family because for the first time, all of us, everyone of all, families are 100% under one roof. Some of you came a long ways, from Washington, D.C., Lansing, Michigan, Albert Lea, Minnesota, Cedar Rapids, Iowa, El Paso, Texas, Phoenix, Arizona, San Francisco, California,

Orange County, my wife's children, - Dr. George Dibs and his wife Mary, brothers Art and Darlyne, and Nicholas,-also George's future son-in-law and his bride and other children.

You know and I know that an occasion like this, for me- 90 years old- or for anyone else like me, may not be repeated very often unless the good Lord will be generous to extend my good credit like he did before. Who knows?

At this time, I would like to take this opportunity to thank everyone of you-my family, the Abraham and Landon family and all family children and their children, as well as our dearest relatives and friends.

I also want to thank our beloved Father Paul Romley for his prayers for me and all the visitations while I was in the hospital. You know that my dear daughter Beatrice took me to the hospital and I never saw any of my family for 20 days. I was in intensive care. So for that I have a few words of thanks to all of you. I was wondering what will become of me at that time without your love and care, without you visitations day in and day out, without our son, Dr. Francis, staying with me 16 days and sleepless nights, without Johnny and his wife Elizabeth who did not go home for 10 days. They also took care of me when I went to the Mayo Clinic. Without our son Joe, and his daily trips to see me, -all the way from Riverside, without our son-in-law George Haddy and his wife Lucille. She took care of my finances with her brother Joe. Without my son-in-law Richard Landon and his wife Juanita's visitation. Without George Shaheen and his wife Donna who came from Phoenix, Arizona to see me. Without my dearest daughter Beatrice and her husband Tony. Their home was open to receive everyone who came to see me and the family. May the Lord grant her and her husband and their family long and healthy lives always. Without our twins, Vernita and Juanita and my sister-in-law Selma's visitation. Without out babies, the twins, Juanita and Vernita. I will never forget the first day I was released from intensive care, and the twins came to my room-they were so hysterical, laughing and crying, when they saw me alive. I'll never forget my wife, Alexandria with her good care for me after I came home. May the lord grant her and everyone of you a long happy and healthy life always.

*YOU KNOW A MAN IS FOOLISH TO DIE WHEN HE HAS A
FAMILY LIKE YOU*

*Now let me tell you how I stand with my doctor with my
health. On June 15th, I took my examination with Dr. Shirey. He
said my heart is good and my lungs are clear. If I want to go to
the old country..that's a different story. The vision on my right eye
is wonderful after the operation. I do my own office work and if I
get stuck, I call on my wife Alexandria for help. My hearing aid
is not so good! I'm trying to get along as good as I can. I invited
the man that sold it to me to come here tonight
but I don't think he came.*

*Now, before I sign off-I would like to tell you about our old
pioneer people who immigrated to this wonderful land of America.
Those people came here with open eyes and good reason, and at
the same time they were blind...because they had to learn
everything, the language, eating, wearing their clothes, and to
conduct themselves like others. They were chased out of some
premises. In spite of all of that and more, they made up their minds
to be Americans and good ones too! with their love and determination to show others that they could do what other's can and
more.*

*They educated their families, establishing businesses.
They are known and respected everywhere. Now they have shown
the world that they can have Doctors, teachers, lawyers, politicians all over the country, including Washington, D.C. Further-
more, they established their religion in North and South America,
including Canada. You can be proud of your Eastern Orthodox
Church. You can be proud of our educated priest in the English and
Arabic languages. Yes, and you can be proud of your old people.
I hope and pray that they will not be forgotten. Please visit them
wherever they are, still alive or resting in peace. You know history
will repeat whatever you do for your old ones- your children will
do for you.*

*Thank you and God bless everyone of you and may the
Lord grant you long lives with health and happiness always.*

*To, Father Paul, Father John, and Deacon George, I want
to thank you for being with us to bless our occasion for my 90th
birthday.*
Your Father   TJ. Haddy"

As Tom sat down after his 'talk' his daughter Vernita rose to read a poem that she had written for the occasion. She read...

"To Dad on his 90th Birthday

Many men have been honored by nations, countries,
states, villages and churches
But the man who is honored by his family
is loved:
There is no greater honor than love
All else is like planting a seed-
without reaping the harvest,
Their coffers may be filled,-
But the heart is empty
Our father, we love you:
May your cup runneth over.

VERNITA
July, 1982

It was a glorious and love filled evening for Tom and he said a silent prayer to his God for the blessing of having his wonderful family. It was night to be remembered.

XXXV

Tom continued to be as active as he could for although his physical health was not as robust as it had been his mind was as clear and as active as some half his age. He continued to be involved in and interested in the Cathedral but others would now carry on the work that he and other visionaries had started many years ago.

On March 8, 1984 Beatrice called and asked if she could pick him up to bring him to her home. When he arrived, Joe and Juanita were there and he had a sense of foreboding for he knew something had happened. Sorrowfully, he was right for they told him as gently as they could that his beloved daughter Lucille had died suddenly of a heart attack. Tom was deeply grieved. He thought of George and Steven and the deep loss that they were suffering. Lucille had been a solid rock for many of them. She had become a fine accountant and Tom had relied on her for many years to keep his finances in order. George had lost his beloved wife and Steven had lost his wonderful mother. She was sixty-six years old and Tom felt that she had so much more living and giving to do and that she had been deprived of the opportunity to do so.

The next few days in preparing for Lucille's funeral were dark and gloomy for Tom as he wondered why his God allowed him to live and had cut short his beloved Lucille's lifespan. He attended her funeral with a heavy heart and sat in the pew of the Cathedral again reading the soothing words of the twenty-third Psalm that was on her memorial card. And he sadly read the words that her family used to remember her wonderful presence...

> *"Perhaps you sent a lovely card,*
> *or sat quietly in a chair*
> *perhaps you sent a funeral spray*
> *if so we saw it there*

perhaps you spoke the kindest words
as any friend could say
perhaps you were not there at all
just thought of us that day
whatever you did to console our hearts
we thank you so much whatever the part"

The sadness continued for Tom for just two months later he joined Beatrice in her grief when she lost her beloved Wadiea.

Tom was rehospitalized and continued to cope with his failing health. He was in and out of the hospital for the next two years and on August 14, 1986 Thomas J. Haddy, Patriarch of the Haddy clan died. On Sunday, August 17th, 1986 at 8:00 p.m., St. Nicholas Cathedral held a special service for one of its founders, patron and beloved friend. They sorrowfully said good-bye. A cryptside service was held on Monday August 18, 1986 at 11:00 a.m. at Forest Lawn Cemetery, Glendale, California. The twenty-third psalm was picked for his memorial card. And in Lebanon his brothers and sister held a special service in his memory.

Tom had passed the legacy from his parents to his children, their children and their children's children- A prescription for living: Honesty, Love, Integrity, Pride and Dedication to family- Love is the basis for all success.

Thomas J. Haddy had stepped across the threshold of God's Eternal Kingdom. Frances was waiting.....

EPILOGUE

The very special circumstances that were part of the lives of the early immigrants to America cannot be fully appreciated by those of us who have not experienced the displacement that comes with immigration. The smallest of functions, such as eating and dressing, became difficult for those who were not familiar with the customs of their adopted land. The language barrier was, for some, a handicap that took years to overcome. All of the strangeness that they experienced caused a sense of inferiority that was intensified when they had to deal with insensitivity from others who were native born. The painful separation from their loved ones can only be understood with the experience. Often these separations were permanent and as in Tom's case the loved one, his father, is never seen again.

The normal strains of every day life were magnified for these early 'settlers' of our land because of their circumstances. Often they had little or no education and had scraped together the money to get here from very meager resources. But as Tom so often said, they had a desire to be good citizens of their adopted land. Their motive for coming here, to give a better life to their children, was so strong that they suffered setbacks and indignity with pride and determination. They raised their families by virtue of hard work and a willingness to do what was considered to be menial work by the native-born people of their adopted country. And most important of all they were, for the most part, people who had deeply held convictions about what the character of man should be. Their moral and social values were solid and because they were these kinds of people they succeeded in making a life for themselves in America. Their contribution to the forming and building of America cannot be measured in terms of dollars. And their most painful and bewildering experience was that they soon realized that in raising their children, they were in fact, raising young Americans. This fact caused them to be fearful that somehow they would lose their ethnic culture and indeed part of their identity. That somehow the cultural gap between their heritage and that of America would drive their children from them. Of course they need not have worried for the future generations of these early immigrants blended the best of two cultural backgrounds and made America what she is. A culturally diverse nation. A cultural diversity that helps her to be the great democracy that she is. And just as Tom's ancestors migrated and helped to build and shape the Lebanon in the earliest days of history Tom and Frances migrated to America and helped to shape and build America. The success of their children and their grandchildren stems directly from the character that was instilled in them by their parents.

J. Johnston

ACKNOWLEDGEMENTS

The author wishes to thank the members of the Haddy family who gave so willingly of their time, memories and thoughts to make the writing of this book possible: Elizabeth and John Haddy, Beatrice Abraham, Thomas Abraham, Wayne Abraham, George Haddy, Steven Haddy, Joseph Haddy, Doris Haddy, Sharon Haddy, Francis Haddy, Theresa Haddy, Richard Haddy, Cheryl Haddy, Carole Froleich, Vernita Haddy, Juanita Landon, and Selma Nemer.

The author wishes to thank Tom's very special friend and priest Father Paul Romley.

And a special thank-you is due to Frances and Theresa Haddy, Beatrice Abraham, Elizabeth Haddy, and Alice Hillen for their time and patience in reading the manuscript and providing the author with valuable comments, suggestions, and corrections.

The author would also like to thank Patricia Johnson for providing her expertise with the Word Perfect Program to make the manuscript suitable to send to the publisher.

A special thank you is due to Kristina Johnston who provided the calligraphic skill for the biblical quote from Psalm 121.

And last but far from least the author wishes to thank her husband Howard, son Kevin, daughter-in-law Kristina, and grandson Jacob for giving her wonderful people to love.

REFERENCES

Fisher, Sydney Nettleton. The Middle East A History. New York: Alfred A. Knopf, 1959

Smith, Harvey H. Nancy W. Al-Any, Donald W. Bernier, Frederica M. Bunge, William Giloane, Joseph G. Jabbra, Peyton Kerr, Suzanne Teleki. Area Handbook for Lebanon. Washington, D.C.: U.S. Government Printing Office, 1974

Herm, Gerhard. The Phoenicians The Purple Empire of the Ancient World. New York: William Morrow and Company, Inc. 1975

Casson, Lionel. The Ancient Mariners. New York: Funk and Wagnalls Publishing Company, Inc., 1959

Munro, Dana Gardner. The Latin American Republics. New York: Appleton-Century Crofts, Inc., 1960

Corey, Helen. The Art of Syrian Cookery. New York, Doubleday and Co., Inc., 1962

St. Nicholas Orthodox Cathedral. Western Region Soyo Parish Life Conference June 29-July 3, 1977, Los Angeles, California

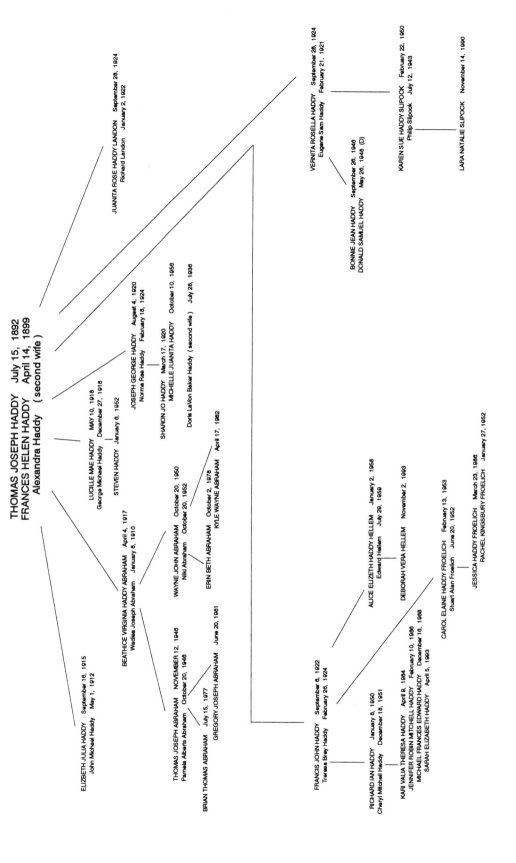

THOMAS JOSEPH HADDY   July 15, 1892
FRANCES HELEN HADDY   April 14, 1899
Alexandra Haddy   (second wife)

ELIZBETH JULIA HADDY   September 16, 1915
John Michael Haddy   May 1, 1912

BEATHICE VIRGINIA HADDY ABRAHAM   April 4, 1917
Wadlea Joseph Abraham   January 8, 1910

THOMAS JOSEPH ABRAHAM   NOVEMBER 12, 1946
Pamela Alberta Abraham   October 20, 1946

BRIAN THOMAS ABRAHAM   July 15, 1977
GREGORY JOSEPH ABRAHAM   June 20, 1981

WAYNE JOHN ABRAHAM   October 20, 1950
Niki Abraham   October 20, 1952

ERIN BETH ABRAHAM   October 2, 1978
KYLE WAYNE ABRAHAM   April 17, 1982

LUCILLE MAE HADDY   MAY 10, 1918
George Michael Haddy   December 27, 1918

STEVEN HADDY   January 8, 1952

JOSEPH GEORGE HADDY   August 4, 1920
Norma Rae Haddy   February 18, 1924

SHARON JO HADDY   March 17, 1920
MICHELLE JUANITA HADDY   October 10, 1956

Doris LaVon Baker Haddy (second wife)   July 28, 1938

JUANITA ROSE HADDY LANDON   September 28, 1924
Richard Landon   January 2, 1922

FRANCIS JOHN HADDY   September 6, 1922
Theresa Brey Haddy   February 28, 1924

RICHARD IAN HADDY   January 8, 1950
Cheryl Mitchell Haddy   December 18, 1951

KARI VALIA THERESA HADDY   April 9, 1984
JENNIFER ROBIN MITCHELL HADDY   February 10, 1986
MICHAEL FRANCES EDWARD HADDY   December 16, 1988
SARAH ELIZABETH HADDY   April 5, 1993

ALICE ELIZETH HADDY HELLEM   January 2, 1958
Edward Hellem   July 29, 1959

DEBORAH VERA HELLEM   November 2, 1993

CAROL ELAINE HADDY FROELICH   February 13, 1953
Stuart Alan Froelich   June 20, 1952

JESSICA HADDY FROELICH   March 23, 1986
RACHEL KINGSBURY FROELICH   January 27, 1952

VERNITA ROSELLA HADDY   September 28, 1924
Eugene Sam Haddy   February 21, 1921

BONNIE JEAN HADDY   September 20, 1946
DONALD SAMUEL HADDY   May 26, 1948 (D)

KAREN SUE HADDY SLIPOCK   February 22, 1950
Philip Slipock   July 12, 1943

LARA NATALIE SLIPOCK   November 14, 1990

Joseph and Tafiha Haddy

Thomas J. Haddy's Siblings and Family

ZARIFE HADDY

GEORGE and Latifi Haddy

- Zahre
- Victoria
- Hanna and Nada Haddy
  - Josette
  - George
  - Mouline
  - Vivian
  - Elie
- Renee
- Michael
- Mounifa
- Antoinette
- Edward
- Sihan
- Hiham

FARIDE HADDY and Hanna Shaheen

- Nada
- Linda
  - David
  - Sonia
  - Elizabeth
- Samla
  - Samira
  - Lorice
  - Samir
  - Toni
- Miguel and Mary
  - Adrianne
  - Danielle
- Janete and Ari
  - Marisa
  - Ricardo
- Gorge and Martha
  - Jorge Jr.
  - Angelo

ELIAS and Sara Haddy

- Wanita and George El Zein
  - Vernita
- Issam and Harla El Laham
  - Elie
  - Eliane
  - Hadi
- Touffana and Joseph Abourjaihy
  - Najla
  - Claude
  - Elie
  - Layla
  - Somar
  - Aziz
- George and Safaa
  - Rina
  - Sandra
- Joseph and Reine
  - David
  - Dima
  - Damer
- Josephene and Habib Abou Maarouf
  - Jad
  - Elie
  - Julie
- Layla and George Aboud
  - Seralene
  - John
  - Elie
- Michael and Rita
  - Violet
- Delal and Bshara El Laham
- Touma and Angela
  - Mario
  - Milad
  - Diana

NICHOLAS and Ramzia Haddy

- Toufic and Martha
  - Morley
  - Marlene
  - Mauricio
  - Marisa
- Assad and Suad
  - Nicolau
  - Emad
  - Caroline
- Merheg and Claire
  - Rola
  - Setta
  - Jorge
- Miguel and Carman
  - Katia
  - Rosana
  - Renata
  - Juliana
- Margarita and Elias
  - Nemer
  - George
  - Joseph
  - Afife
- Nazir and Eid
  - Jean
  - Elie